ALTERNATE AMERICAN HISTORY 101

ABE LINCOLN, HUEY LONG, AMELIA EARHART, FDR, MARILYN MONROE, RFK, AND THE JFK ASSASSINATION

YOUR FIRST PRESIDENTIAL BRIEFING

BILL TRUELS, MD

What if everything you knew
Turned out to be untrue?
Is there an alternate Universe
Where space and time reverse?

My whole world view would change –
My life would rearrange!
I'd have a whole new perspective
Of the Universal Directive!

TABLE OF CONTENTS

PROLOGUE

Many of the world's mysteries
Are not explained by official history –
The reason they are never solved
Is because the government was involved!

Each new President is given a confidential Presidential briefing that provides the "lowdown" or true accounting of American history. Former President Barack Obama stated that, after his first Presidential intelligence briefing, he was tempted to jump out the window, as he listened in disbelief at what he was being told. Most of the major events in American history have been falsely reported, and at times contrived, in order to protect the assets of those involved and achieve the Greater Good.

Some of these accounts were told to me by fellow surgeons and colleagues, who I worked with on a daily basis. These men were department chairmen, well respected in their community, and, in one case, president of the American Podiatry Association.

Throughout my life, I've been confronted with conflicting information about major events. This paper represents my best effort at resolving those dilemmas. I encourage each reader to not casually accept what they read or hear at face value, but rather to embark on their own search for truth. These accounts are the results of my personal search for understanding the world around me.

Here then, is my best analysis at what your first Presidential briefing might disclose!

Bill Truels, M.D.

INTRODUCTION

YOUR FIRST PRESIDENTIAL BRIEFING

WELCOME, MR. PRESIDENT!
FOR YOUR EYES ONLY
ABOVE TOP SECRET/MAJIC 12

"Mr. President – this may come as a shock – but many of the major events in American history have been intentionally falsely portrayed. These include:

1. Assassination of Abe Lincoln
2. The assassination of Zachary Taylor
3. The assassination of William Harrison
4. The assassination of Wm McKinley
5. The Lindbergh kidnapping
6. The assassination of Huey Long
7. The Amelia Earhart mystery
8. Pearl Harbor 'surprise attack'
9. The death of Joe Kennedy Jr
10. The illness and assassination of FDR
11. The murder of Marilyn Monroe
12. The assassination of John Kennedy
13. The assassination of Martin Luther King
14. The assassination of Robert Kennedy
15. The assassination of JFK Jr
16. The existence of UFOs and extraterrestrial Beings

"These historical misrepresentations were all done for Good Reason – to protect the assets of the people involved and guide the Ship of State! I'll explain why as we go along!"

The clever Conspirators betrayed one of their own,
To placate the People in their Grief
But the Betrayer would not tell his tale!
"For if I am not loyal to my own People, to whom shall I be true?"
And the Secret did die with him, for he knew not whom to trust!

ABRAHAM LINCOLN

"Welcome, Mr. President. Congratulations on your victory!"

"Let me ask you—have you ever wanted to know all the answers? Have you ever felt like you weren't being told the truth about our American history?"

"Well, I'm here to give your first Presidential briefing – just call me Holden Coalfield. Mr. President, I'm here to tell you everything you want to know but were afraid to ask!"

I'll do most of the talking. I'm going to warn you that you're not going to believe most of what I have to tell you. This meeting is all about honesty. But it's important that you at least hear what I have to say, even if it takes a while to sink in over the next few years!"

"Oh, you've talked to Presidential scholars – very good, Mr. President. They teach what we call a counterfeit history. You see, history is written by the victors, and the victors don't want you to know about the skeletons in the closet – every country has them, you know!"

"Archeologist Graham Hancock talks about 'a hidden hand in human history' that limits our ability to consider alternate explanations – a sort of 'intellectual territory' that gives historians a certain reluctance to correct the established explanations!"

"The reason, Mr. President, that we Intel boys want to tell you about the skeletons in the closet is to warn you, so that you don't become a skeleton yourself! But more about that later."

"Try not to jump out of the window when you hear all this. We had one President that entertained such thoughts – maybe he was joking – I don't know."

"What I have to tell you is not a pretty picture. Our Intel boys have made a few mistakes, I'll grant you. But it was all for the Greater Good. I'm very proud of our country!"

"First, let me give you a disqualifier. Mr. President, do you know what a Rumor is?"

"That's right! A Rumor is a verbal account, passed from person to person, that may or may not be true!"

"What I'm going to give you, Mr. President, is a series of Rumors – an antithetical version of American History that you won't find in any history books."

"I can't tell you which of these Rumors are true – your security level isn't high enough! Presidential Security is ten levels below Cosmic Clearance – that's reserved for the CIA and Secret Space Program corporations like Lockheed Martin. I can only tell you that some of these Rumors might be true!"

"From a practical standpoint, you might assume that all of these Rumors are true – that way, you won't be caught unprepared!"

"If I tell you, for example, that extraterrestrial beings exist and fly antigravity devices, you won't be caught off guard if one of them lands on the White House lawn. That's just a Rumor, mind you, and that's all I can say at this time, but be prepared for some rather outlandish Rumors!"

"You're asking about Abraham Lincoln?"

"You want to go that far back?"

"Well, O.K. – let's first go a little farther back – to 1857 – when the New Orleans Mardi Gras Mystick Krewe of Comus was formed and met at Pope's pharmacy – today we call them the 'Deep State.' The best account comes from Mimi Eustis, who tape recorded her father's deathbed confession, Samuel Todd Churchill, concerning the founding of the Mystick Krewe of Comus in 1857 and his membership in Chapter 322 – known as the Brotherhood of Death. Each member was required to memorize their history!"

This was a group of bankers with international ties, politicians, and ne'er do wells who supported slavery and opposed President Buchanan. During a meeting at the National Hotel in 1857, arsenic was sprinkled in the sugar at the Northerners table – though Buchanan survived, 38 Northerners died, while none of the Southerners became ill! The nausea, vomiting, and bloody diarrhea were blamed on bad water – no conspiracy here!"

In the late 1800s, Washington's National Hotel was the place to be seen.

"The other secret club worth mentioning is Skull and Bones, formed in 1832 by William Russell, at Yale University, also with international banking ties, and with a key partner named Caleb Cushing. This group also supported slavery. Two Presidents, who opposed admitting Texas and California as slave states, also died of arsenic poisoning – William Henry Harrison in 1841 and Zachary Taylor in 1850 – courtesy of Caleb Cushing!"

"In the case of President Harrison, they first called it pneumonia after giving his inaugural speech one month earlier. Three weeks later they called it typhus, when he developed gastroenteritis, including bloody diarrhea, nausea, vomiting and crampy abdominal pain, as well as headaches and leg cramps. But these symptoms are also seen with arsenic poisoning – so called 'inheritance powder!' His symptoms worsened dramatically after eating dinner on March 27, 1841 – only eight days before his death! His big mistake was calling in Dr. Frederick May and Dr. William Eustis, a British spy, to treat his ailments! John Tyler, who became President, was a Freemason, a pro-secessionist, and a slave-owner!"

"President Zachary Taylor developed the same symptoms – nausea, vomiting, bloody diarrhea – after drinking a juice cocktail on July 4, 1850, and died five days later. Once again, typhus was implicated and blamed on dirty sewer water near the White House. But Professor Clara Rising from the University of Florida was suspicious of arsenic poisoning. A neutron activation study in 1991 on Taylor's hair sample was weakly positive for arsenic at 1.9 ppm vs the Mayo Clinic norm of 1.0 ppm. Professor Rising was roundly ridiculed for raising a conspiracy theory. But significant arsenic doesn't show up in hair samples for two weeks, and President Taylor died only five days after his arsenic ingestion! We make sure that people who search for the truth are roundly ridiculed – that protects us, you know!"

"So, you see, there was quite a leadup to the Lincoln assassination in 1865. Slavery was one of the motivations, but the international bankers in this group were furious at Lincoln's use of 'Greenbacks' to finance the Civil War, which threatened to break the power of the international bankers."

"You want to know more about the Illuminati, Mr. President? That's just a fancy name for a group of international connivers at the top who think they're special – intellectuals, bankers, spies, politicians, corporate execs, ne'er do wells, who think they know best, and keep a special book in their library! I mean, you've got to be suspicious of any group that goes around calling themselves, 'The Enlightened Ones'! Joe Kennedy said there's about a hundred people who run this country, and that's probably an exaggeration! Jim Marrs writes all about the Illuminati."

"You don't take the Illuminati seriously, Mr. President?"

"You have to take them seriously, Mr. President, because they kill people! They even have a ceremony they practice every year, called, 'The Killing of the King' ritual – it's like a play that they act out, just to keep them in shape! They think of themselves like actors on a stage – except, every once in a while, it's the real deal – it's not Shakespeare anymore!"

"Now, a secret group within the Mystick Krewe of Comus included Albert Pike, Judah Benjamin and John Slidell, and was now meeting at the Pickwick Club in New Orleans. John Wilkes Booth is a member of the Knights of the Golden Circle, founded by Albert Pike. In March, 1864, John Wilkes Booth performed at the St. Charles Theatre in New Orleans, and met with Pike, Benjamin and Slidell. They formulated plans to assassinate Lincoln, and John Wilkes Booth became the secret King of the Mystic Krewe of Comus! You should be aware, Mr. President, that there is a certain Spartan tradition of comradery and personal bonding within these secret societies!"

"Captain James William Boyd, a Confederate Secret Service agent who resembled Booth, and originally worked under Benjamin, was to be the designated patsy, and was killed in the tobacco barn 12 days later, and Admiral G. W. Baird, who had met Booth earlier, would certify the body of Captain Boyd to be John Wilkes Booth aboard the ship Montauk at the naval yard in Washington. The body was then dumped into a sinkhole used to dump dead horses!"

"So, you see, John Wilkes Booth – a famous actor in his day – was also a spy – he carried a decoder that was in the hands of fewer than one in 10,000 people. He was also a political activist and Confederate sympathizer – part of a conspiracy that also tried to kill the Secretary of State, William Seward that night!"

"Now, Lincoln is in Ford theater, his security is compromised when his security guard takes a break, and John Wilkes Booth shoots Lincoln with a .44 caliber Deringer pistol, jumps down onto the stage, sustains a fractured leg, and escapes on horseback!"

"Twelve days later, a man that looks like Booth, is shot and killed in a burning tobacco barn at the Garrett farm in Port Royal, Virginia."

"You're right, Mr. President, that's not the end of the story."

"A man named David George, who previously used an alias, John St. Helens, and worked as a painter who liked to quote Shakespeare, takes cyanide around 1903 in Enid, Oklahoma and claims on his deathbed that he was John Wilkes Booth!"

"A computerized digital analysis has been performed comparing photos – Booth's photo has a 99% match with David George and a 97% match with John St. Helens – police consider a 95% match to be significant!"

"Several researchers are refused permission by historians to obtain DNA from the John Wilkes Booth gravesite, or to check for a broken leg. One researcher, named Nate Orlowek, makes the statement:

'If we prove the man killed in the barn wasn't John Wilkes Booth, then no historical fact will be safe from further examination. It would fundamentally change the way history and contemporary events are viewed. . . The transcendent importance is the importance of knowing our own history, and knowing it accurately.'"

"You want to tell the truth, Mr. President? Hardly a good idea – it's important to protect our assets. We're like magicians, you know – a good magician never gives away his secrets!"

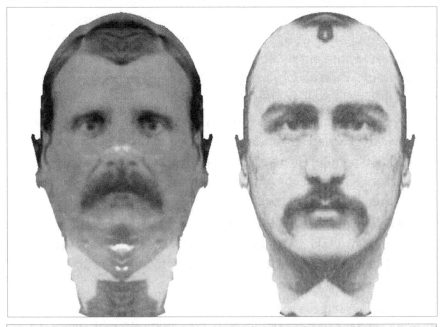

JOHN ST. HELEN   **JOHN WILKES BOOTH**

Philadelphia Inquirer 4/15/19 with photos from the Discovery Channel

Thus, did the Spymasters and the Underworld
Kill those who would speak out against them.
For the murder of one opponent silences ten others!

SENATOR HUEY LONG

"Let's get to more modern times, Mr. President – you need to know about the Huey Long assassination. Why, if it wasn't for the successful Huey Long assassination, the assassinations of JFK, MLK, RFK and JFK Jr might never have happened!"

"True, the Lincoln assassination used compromised security and a patsy in the tobacco barn. But the Huey Long assassination demonstrated the successful use of a patsy, with or without a gun, the compromising of the security guards, the intimidation of witnesses, and the control of the news media, as well as the FBI director pulling a few strings, both before and after the assassination – that's right, J. Edgar Hoover played a role in most of them, but was not the prime motivator – more of a facilitator-as you'll see!"

"Let me first explain that these Illuminati-Skull and Bones activists – today we call them the 'Deep State'. They were using the Masons as a cover for these New World Order international banking elites. But it wasn't just about the money – there was a sense of globalism vs nationalism – that we are all citizens of the world and the idea was that each country must yield to this new world scheme!"

"Those who resisted would suffer the consequences. Illuminati doctors played a vital role in the death of President James Garfield in 1881, who lived two months after being shot, and President William McKinley in 1901, who lived eight days after being shot!"

"McKinley had been in favor of a new canal project through Nicaragua, as was the Congress. When Teddy Roosevelt assumed the Presidency, he convinced Congress to continue the Panama Canal Project, which the French had started, by paying off J.P. Morgan and the French bankers 40 million dollars! The assassination of President McKinley by 'anarchist' Leon Czolgosz netted the European bankers 100 billion dollars in today's money! Teddy Roosevelt later became the Secret King of the Mardi Gras Mystick Krewe of Comus!"

"That's right, Mr. President – the bodies are piling up! The lesson here is that a good President will do what he is told!"

"Mr. President, the assassination of Huey Long showed what can be done when a tremendously popular leader comes along, but with the wrong message. Do you realize that the cars were backed up 80 miles – all the way from New Orleans to Baton Rouge – for the Huey Long funeral in 1935?"

"In Senator Long's case, his bombastic behavior was disliked by both Republicans and Democrats in Congress, as well as FDR himself. FDR called Huey Long, a firm isolationist, the second most dangerous man in America! His attack on the oil companies and his 'Share the Wealth' platform was nothing more than a communist strategy and a recipe for disaster!"

"Something had to be done to the upstart 42-year-old Senator Long; he was a serious challenge to FDR in 1936, just like Lindbergh had been a potential challenge in 1932! Enter the Mystic Krewe of Comus and the Skull and Bones chapter at the Tulane University Medical School and Dr. Rudolph Matas, who sends a bright young surgeon activist, who speaks French and German, to travel to Europe and join the Illuminati – Dr. Carl Austin Weiss. Dr. Matas also selects Yvonne Pavy, who later marries Dr. Weiss, to travel to Paris and meet the Illuminati."

"Now, Dr. Weiss's father-in-law was Judge Pavy, whose district was being gerrymandered by Huey Long – providing a motive for his son-in-law, Dr Weiss, to attack Huey Long. I'm sure Dr. Matas was heart-broken when the Illuminati picked his most brilliant and favorite student, Dr. Carl Weiss, to play the role of patsy! But Dr. Matas is described as having a consuming hatred for Huey Long and notified Dr. Weiss of his upcoming role."

"Then, on the night of September 8, 1935 in Baton Rouge, Dr. Weiss is ordered to throw a punch at Senator Huey Long. He resists at first – do you really need a doctor to throw a punch? But then he is threatened with the death of his newborn son, like Charles Lindbergh. When you join a secret branch of a society like the Minutemen, you take an oath that you will perform whatever you are asked – at risk of death! It's interesting that the older men pick the younger men – those with less seniority – to be the patsy! Dr. Weiss somberly kisses his wife good-by and heads for the Capitol."

"Dr. Weiss may have been told that he's going to walk away – all he'll do is throw a punch – a scuffle will ensue, then the bodyguards will 'accidentally' shoot Huey Long – end of story. Dr. Weiss even schedules surgery the next day – but then the bodyguards take turns finishing off Dr. Weiss with one shot to the eye and 61 more rounds as he sits on the floor, without a gun!"

"Dr. Weiss's gun is later retrieved from his car and the .32 caliber Browning pistol, which disappears for 56 years in the police chief's daughter's possession, is blamed for the .38 and .45 slugs found in Huey. It's later revealed that one of the bodyguards is on J. Edgar's payroll! Dr.Ochsner later states his belief that the bodyguards killed Huey Long!"

"And J. Edgar just happened to be on the phone at the Louisiana State Capitol in Baton Rouge when Huey was shot. It turned out that Dr. Weiss had left both his wallet and his gun in his car, so J. Edgar provided Dr. Weiss's name over the phone – Hoover believed it was very important to get the name out quickly to an unsuspecting and traumatized public!"

"Dr. Long's physician, Dr. Arthur Vidrine, a family practitioner, just happens to be in Baton Rouge that Sunday night and somehow is allowed to take charge of the surgical management. While Vidrine is portrayed as a supporter of Huey Long and a Rhodes scholar, he is also a member of the Tulane Skull and Bones Illuminati. The family practitioner then dismisses the surgeon, Dr. Cook, from the operating room, who is reluctant to leave. A decision to re-explore is cancelled, and Huey Long slowly bleeds to death over the next 30 hours from a retroperitoneal bleed, after receiving only four units of blood, uttering, 'Please don't let me die!'"

"One Mafioso, Frank Costello, who knew Huey Long, claimed they could have saved him, but the doctors had their orders to let him die!"

"FDR is crowned King of the Mystic Krewe in 1937 and knighted into the 33rd level. J. Edgar Hoover, already at the 33rd level, was later crowned King of the Mystic Krewe of Comus!"

"What's that you say, Mr. President – shooting innocent people for their political beliefs isn't right? Well, I was a member of Hoover's 'Squad' as we called it – today they call it the 'wet works division', and we were active during the turbulent sixties! I actually had to work with some of those Nazis they brought over from Germany after the war – Operation Paperclip – they weren't all scientists, you know!"

"But I never killed an anti-war activist that didn't have it coming! I once posed as a plumber for two months in a college dorm, just to get a bead on this anti-war communist leader – those college kids actually made fun of me as I fixed their toilets! I was tempted to ram a Sloan valve down this one arrogant kid's throat, but it was J. Edgar Hoover that taught me self-control – only kill your assignment – that's what he taught me!"

"You're asking about the Lindbergh kidnapping, Mr. President? I wouldn't go there if I were you! Charles Lindbergh was an aviation hero with tremendous popularity – and Presidential ambitions – but he was a strict isolationist and, like the Rockefeller bankers, he supported that anti-Semite, Adolph Hitler, before Pearl Harbor! Most documentaries about Charles Lindbergh portray him as socially awkward and apolitical."

"But Lindbergh, like Henry Ford, was opposed to going to war against Germany. Lindbergh was warned about his isolationist policies, and his initial support of Germany, but to no avail. His 20-month – old son, Charles Jr. was kidnapped and killed in the spring of 1932, with his body found two months later!"

"The details? I'm still not allowed to talk about this! I've seen the 'you no toucha' files on the Lindbergh kidnapping – they're three feet thick!"

"Alright, alright – I'll do a limited hangout and let you be the detective. The first clue is that FDR and J. Edgar had Lucky Lindy under surveillance – that's right, phone taps, personal surveillance, you name it – they viewed Lucky Lindy – the most popular man in the country – as the most dangerous man in the country – why, he might even run for President in 1932! If Little Lindy caught a cold, they knew about it before the doctor!"

"Wild Bill Donovan of the OSS even shadowed Lindbergh in Germany and wrote disapprovingly to FDR about Lindbergh's multiple trips – even awards – from pre-war Germany! Don't forget that the Rockefellers were Hitler's pre-war financial backers at that time!"

"The second clue is that Richard Hauptmann, the German carpenter, was framed-they even caricatured him with a false nickname – Bruno!"

"Now use the gray matter here, Mr. President. If Richard Hauptmann is innocent, then you've got to look at Isidore Fisch, Hauptmann's banker friend. Hauptmann states that Isidore gave him the box with the numbered gold certificate ransom bills, which had been used in the Lindbergh kidnapping, for past debts. Isidore then sailed back to Germany with his intimate friend, Henry Uhlig in 1933 – talk about a setup!"

"FDR and J. Edgar saw it as a twofer – sabotage Lindy's political ambitions and vilify the Germans at a time when right wing political activists were being persecuted in Germany, amid war rumblings in Europe!"

"The third clue, Mr. President, is that J. Edgar, while claiming the Mafia didn't exist, used the Mafia for domestic assassinations – what you would call a symbiotic relationship!"

"You ask if this was an inside job? Well, if the Lindbergh house staff were involved, one of them would have been offered money for inside knowledge. Isidore Fisch, Hauptmann's banker friend, was seen several times at the Ice Cream Parlor before the kidnapping with Violet Sharp, the Lindbergh housekeeper. This exculpatory evidence should have re-opened the case, but the government refused Mrs. Hauptmann's request in 1982, and still refuses to declassify thousands of documents after 90 years!"

When Violet left the house at 8:30 pm, the kidnappers made their move, as Charles was quite strict that the boy not be disturbed between 7:30 and 10:00 pm! The unlocked window on the second-floor nursery was no accident! Lindbergh recalls hearing a sound around 9 p.m. When the body of Charles Jr. was found two months later, Violet had a tearful private meeting with Betty Gow, the nanny. Violet blamed herself for Little Lindy's death and died from cyanide poisoning the next day!"

"Isidor Fisch was a political activist with a secret FBI file, who was strongly opposed to Lindbergh's isolationist policies and his pre-war support for Germany – not the frail man portrayed in the press! Let's face it, Mr. President, if the United States hadn't entered the war, Hitler would have taken over Europe and millions more Jews and political opponents would have been sent to the gas chambers! Isidore Fisch was one of history's unacknowledged heroes! Officially, he conveniently died of an unusually rapid tuberculosis in Germany in 1934 – before the Hauptmann trial! Unofficially, he died in an Israeli kibbutz in 1969! His gravestone stated, 'Er lebte nur fur die Seinen' – he lived only for his people!"

"We all felt bad about Hauptmann going to the electric chair – all he had to do was confess to a crime he didn't commit, like James Earl Ray, the Martin Luther King patsy, and he could have spent the rest of his life in prison! That would have ended all the second-guessing by the conspiracy theorists! Even Hoover felt bad about that!"

"There you have it – the 'Crime of the Century' may have been the cover-up of the century! And it'll take another hundred years for the people to be told!'"

"After Pearl Harbor, Lindbergh tried to enlist in the Army Air Force but was famously refused! The last thing the establishment needed was Lindbergh returning as a war hero in 1945 and running for President! He actually became a civilian fighter pilot, flew fifty missions, and shot down one Japanese Zero! But you'll never hear about that! And they're still vilifying Lindbergh today – claiming he kidnapped his own child!"

"Patton, Mr. President? Why does everybody ask about General George Patton? Well, that's true, he was a very popular General – a potential Presidential candidate for 1948 – before his untimely death in a freakish car accident near Heidelberg, Germany in December, 1945. Patton had a dangerous charisma – he once commanded a crowd of 20,000 American citizens on a moment's notice! But he was a pain in the ass! He was a potential rival for Truman in 1948 and Eisenhower in 1952, neither of whom liked him. You couldn't count on him to follow orders. He was a loose cannon!"

"Both Lindbergh and Patton were more sympathetic to the post-war Germans and opposed Morganthau's harsh 'industrial disarmament' plan for Germany. Patton was anxious to take Berlin and Prague instead of the Russians, but General Eisenhower sent the gasoline to General Montgomery instead! Even Forrestal and JFK, who visited Germany after the war, were amazed at the destruction and rape of Berlin by the Russians!"

"We tapped Patton's phone lines, you know – that's public knowledge-we kept a watch on our own General! Wild Bill Donovan in the OSS gave the order, which came from FDR's Brain Trust. That hunting trip on the day before his European departure was a clever ruse to deprive him of his usual security. That Army GMC truck driver drove directly into his car – and no one was prosecuted – they even classified the records! General Patton was the only one injured. He lived for 12 more days until a special visitor arrived at the hospital!"

"The Morganthau Plan, which Patton claimed was too harsh on the post-war Germans, eventually proved unworkable and was replaced by the more compassionate Marshall Plan in 1948, but by then hundreds of thousands of former German soldiers and civilians had died in the Rheinberg camps."

"Documents, Mr. President? You'd like to see the documents? What I'm providing to you is a verbal history, passed through the ages. My favorite historian is Josephus – historians denied his accounts for centuries about a mass suicide at Masada, only to have archeologists confirm his veracity!"

"Documents are for Presidential historians, Mr. President, who twist and weave their accounts to satisfy the victors!"

"One last note of irony, Mr. President – while Huey's 'Share the Wealth' program was ridiculed, as well as his attack on the oil companies, nobody seemed to mind when the state of Alaska began distributing annual oil royalties to every man, woman and child who was an Alaskan citizen!"

"The major lesson for you in all of this, Mr. President, is don't think that your popularity will save you from the bankers and the Intel boys if you're charting the wrong course! They've got six ways to Sunday to straighten you out!"

"Yes, Mr. President – Huey Long's death was quite a shock to the American public – the cars were lined up for 80 miles-all the way from New Orleans and along Lake Pontchartrain to Prairieville to Baton Rouge – but it was for the Greater Good!"

"These explanations, Mr. President, are not intended for the General Public – we must protect our assets, you know!"

Now King John had many Lovers,
for he loved Life and the Pleasures of Life!
But his Enemies schemed to use them against Him!
Thus arose the Universal Duality-
One life in Public, One in Private!

MARILYN MONROE

"Why do all the new Presidents ask about Marilyn Monroe – a movie star – I can't figure that out. It's not a very happy picture, and perhaps it's better left unsaid."

"There you go, Mr. President, talking about ghosts again. Alright, if there is such a thing, the ghost of Marilyn Monroe would want her reputation restored – you know she didn't commit suicide, don't you?"

"Alright, let me start from the beginning. First of all, the world should know that Marilyn Monroe was a patriot – she loved going on those USO trips with Bob Hope overseas to rally the troops – the troops loved her!"

"And she was one of the greatest actresses of all time – everybody agrees on that."

"What a lot of people don't know is that Marilyn did a lot of favors for the CIA. She was smarter than a lot of people give her credit, and she loved to meet world leaders. She agreed to wear a wire on some of these liaisons, such as the Shah of Iran, as a favor to the CIA for possible future blackmail use."

"Now, let's fast forward. President John Kennedy was what you call a 'rounder' – he loved his women! And Marilyn Monroe was one of them. One FBI agent named Robert Fitzpatrick tells the story of JFK sneaking out of the White House for one of his liaisons. J. Edgar Hoover has all the girlfriend's houses wired for sound and they detect JFK's location. The FBI then phones the Secret Service, and they come running over like the Keystone Cops with the 'nuclear football' that has all the missile launch codes, and is never supposed to be out of the President's sight!"

"Needless to say, some Secret Service agents didn't hold JFK in the highest regard, especially when they were out of town with the President, and they had to find girlfriends. Those naked pool parties at the White House weren't exactly a hit with the Secret Service either! You'd have to think some of that behavior affected their loyalty – especially when they got to Dealey Plaza, but that's another story!"

"O.K., Mr. President, sorry for the digression. Sometimes I tend to gossip!"

"To make a long story short, Marilyn is 36 years old, has another fling with JFK and gets pregnant. Like most movie stars before the age of the birth control pill, and during the era of the casting couch, she's had previous abortions. But this time Marilyn wants to have the baby – she wants to raise the child, even if it's on her own! This presents a problem – this represents a possible scandal for JFK's reelection prospects!"

"Now, Robert Kennedy steps in – for all intents and purposes, RFK is John's campaign manager, close brother, protector, guardian angel – you name it. RFK starts dating Marilyn, as her best friend Jeanne Carmen relates. They have an affair and, in one of Hoover's FBI tapes, RFK even offers to marry Marilyn at some time in the future – but now is not the time!"

"Marilyn is pressured to have the abortion. There's a big get-together in Reno with all the powers that be – Peter Lawford, Frank Sinatra, Chicago mafia boss Sam Giancana, even Robert Kennedy, who temporarily makes peace with Giancana, despite his War on Organized Crime."

"Even Marilyn's role in the movie "Something's Got to Give" is threatened until Dean Martin steps in and threatens to resign if Marilyn is fired!"

"They all offer Marilyn money – anything. The question of killing Marilyn Monroe arises for the first time – a verbal threat made by Sam Giancana if Marilyn fails to act. So, Marilyn reluctantly agrees. She gets out of the hospital, and now RFK won't speak to her and angrily tells her not to call him anymore!"

"Marilyn is distraught. Tape recorded phone conversations by the FBI reveal Marilyn threatening to talk about the existence of UFOs and alien Beings. But James Jesus Angleton of the CIA is paranoid about anyone discussing the greatest secret since the Manhattan Project."

"Keep in mind that the CIA is not allowed to carry out domestic assassinations. But before Allen Dulles retired from the CIA, as described by Michael Salla, he issued a mandate that approved 'wet works' on UFO whistleblowers. So, James Jesus Angleton orders Marilyn's demise, and gives the order to the Mafia!"

"But there's a catch here. Wouldn't it be simpler to simply ridicule Marilyn for making such outlandish claims that UFOs and aliens really exist? Who's going to believe Marilyn anyway?"

"Angleton's real target is his nemesis, Robert Kennedy who, along with JFK, has promised to destroy the CIA! What if Marilyn were suicided right after a visit from RFK – that would be a scandal to end RFK's career, his War on Crime, and his future hopes for President!"

"Now, Giancana, the Chicago crime boss, has been angry at Marilyn for dating his arch-rival, RFK, who has now resumed his surveillance on Giancana. RFK ranks Giancana Numero Uno for his War on Crime. Like Angleton, Giancana relishes the opportunity to kill Marilyn, if he can somehow tarnish RFK's reputation in the process!"

"Giancana, through Johnny Rosselli and Marilyn's friend, Jeanne Carmen, pressures Marilyn to get RFK to personally apologize to her at her Brentwood home. Marilyn replies that Bobby will never come – he won't even answer the phone! Then Marilyn is told to tell RFK that their liaisons have been tape recorded, and that she will release them if he doesn't personally apologize!"

"So, Bobby is maneuvered by Angleton and Giancana into going to Marilyn's Brentwood home. He arrives with Peter Lawford and starts rummaging around in her home – he finds J. Edgar Hoover's wires and all hell breaks loose! He accuses Marilyn of blackmail, but Marilyn pleads with Bobby that she has no tapes. Marilyn is telling the truth – unknown to Marilyn, tapes were actually being recorded in a nearby van by the FBI. The wires had been secretly placed during a renovation project. Bobby is furious and storms out, leaving Marilyn in tears."

"Now Giancana's hit team arrives from Chicago with one CIA hit man, who provides the fatal barbiturate/Nembutal suppository, which is wrapped in cheesecloth so that it can be removed once the fatal dose is administered. This hit man later admits on his deathbed that he has killed 50 men for the CIA and one woman – Marilyn Monroe. The involvement of the CIA protects Giancana from disclosure. And all the while the FBI is listening in a truck outside, but has been ordered to stand down!"

"The hit team threatens Marilyn's house lady, Eunice Murray, and tells her that they will kill her and her son if she reveals their presence. They order her to tell the police about Bobby's visit that night. Angleton's and Giancana's goal was to end RFK's career – and his War on Crime – with the scandal of Marilyn's purported suicide over RFK!"

"Are you with me so far, Mr. President? Because here things take another twist!"

"No, Mr. President. Marilyn never calls Peter Lawford and tells him, with dying breath, 'You're a swell guy!' By now, Marilyn is unconscious."

"Eunice Murray, the house lady, calls Peter Lawford instead of the police! This ruins the entire trap! Peter Lawford rushes back to Marilyn's house with RFK. Bobby rides in the ambulance to the hospital and says a prayer for Marilyn, who is on her final breaths!"

"You're not going to believe this, but after Marilyn dies, they return Marilyn to her house and clean things up a bit. Marilyn had hemorrhoids and there was some blood on the sheets from the rather bulky suppository, so when the police finally are called, they wonder why Eunice Murray is washing the sheets. They also notice that Marilyn has been dead for several hours!"

"The decision is made by Lawford and RFK that they will stick with the suicide story, and Eunice Murray will deny RFK's visit that night, as well as the actions of Giancana's henchmen. Dozens of people at the hospital, even the ambulance driver, had to be sworn to secrecy."

"RFK makes a frantic call to J. Edgar Hoover. RFK pleads with J. Edgar and promises to drop efforts to remove J. Edgar as FBI director. But RFK has another trump card – Eunice has told him that the Mafia was involved, that Marilyn didn't commit suicide, and that the FBI stood down while monitoring in their surveillance van outside – this implicates foreknowledge by J. Edgar in the plot. Hoover is pressured to participate in the cover-up, and takes over the Marilyn Monroe investigation. The Los Angeles police and Daryl Gates are pressured to stand down and phone records are compromised. All's well that ends well!"

"There's one other casualty, Mr. President, from all this – her name is Eugenia Pappas – a young Greek hair stylist from Chicago that's part of my extended Greek family. She made the mistake of befriending a Mafia member, Frank Schweihs, who was part of the Marilyn Monroe hit team- he even bought her a new car! Eugenia talks about the Chicago hit team that flew out of Palwaukee Airport and attended a party on the night of Marilyn's murder. Giancana gave orders to Schweihs for her to be silenced, and she was found months later in the frozen Chicago river with a gunshot to the chest!"

"The coroner, Mr. President? Yes, well that's complicated. Dr. Noguchi notes that Marilyn's stomach is empty, despite the high drug levels, which is very unusual for a pill overdose. He notices a discoloration in the rectum. But he concludes that Marilyn died from a 'probable suicide' – end of story!"

"A good conspiracy story, you say, Mr. President? Too convoluted to be true? That's exactly what we want the public to think! You see, part of disinformation, Mr. President is to occasionally tell the truth, like you just heard – then we let the professional skeptics in the media take over and talk about another preposterous conspiracy theory. It protects us all!"

"The only real victim here, besides Eugenia Pappas, is Marilyn Monroe – her presumed suicide sullies her reputation and she is portrayed as a hopeless, depressed druggie. Angleton fails to end RFK's career, and Giancana fails to end RFK's war on crime. But J. Edgar gets another Kennedy scandal – another trump card to pull in case his job as FBI director is threatened!"

"One last note that Jean Carmen, Marilyn's friend relates. Years later, Giancana is under police protection in 1975 at his Oak Park home in Chicago, scheduled to testify before the Church Committee. Johnny Roselli gets the contract and James Files relates that Roselli had arrived at O'hare airport that morning."

"Roselli, a long-time friend of Marilyn, tells Jeanne Carmen that he relishes killing Giancana that night, as he cooks sausage and peppers, for Giancana had accepted the contract for his Chicago hit team to kill the innocent Marilyn in an unsuccessful attempt to end RFK's career! Roselli angrily yells at Giancana as he lays dying on the floor!"

"Sounds like a soap opera, you say? You're right, Mr. President – life is a soap opera and we're all players on a stage!"

"As usual, Mr. President, this explanation is not intended for the General Public and must be labeled just another Rumor!"

Thus, did the Rulers ask,
"How can you tell the Reformers from the Disrupters,
Good from Evil, and Right from Wrong?"
Must the Son pay for the sins of the Father?

JOHN F. KENNEDY JR., RFK, JFK, JOSEPH KENNEDY JR.

"You want to know about JFK Jr., Mr. President? Why?"

"You think there was a conspiracy?"

"You'd best not go there, Mr. President. Some things are better left unsaid."

"You don't need to know the details, Mr. President."

"The real motivation for the JFK Jr. assassination, Mr. President, was the same motive for the RFK assassination. You see, after John was killed in 1963, RFK literally moved in with Jackie – the two commiserated together over JFK's death. Bobbie was like a father to Carolyn and John Jr."

"Polls showed Bobbie was the presidential favorite in 1968. Then he starts talking about pulling out of Viet Nam and reopening the JFK investigation when he becomes President. I was there when he packed the auditorium at Indiana University in the spring of 1968- I even shook his hand! So, we had to pull the plug."

"That's right, Mr. President, Sirhan, the purported assassin, who was a horse trainer and had big gambling debts at the racetrack, fired a whole bunch of shots. But Sirhan never got closer than five feet to RFK in the Ambassador Hotel kitchen, thanks to Roosevelt Grier, his bodyguard."

"Then the forensic pathologist, Dr. Cyril Wecht, comes along and determines that powder burns on RFK's temple show that the fatal head shot was fired only three inches behind RFK's right ear! It turns out that Thane Cesar, the bodyguard standing directly behind RFK, was a last-minute change by Robert Maheu, who owns the Ace Detective Agency, and formerly worked for the CIA. Maheu was known for his Mafia contacts through Johnny Roselli. Cesar is Maheu's only member of the Ace Detective Agency. Crucial pictures taken by a college student in the kitchen were confiscated by the Los Angeles police and later lost!"

"Coincidences, Mr. President? No – at this level coincidences are manufactured to look like coincidences – that's part of the magic! And if you doubt that, we'll call you a conspiracy theorist – that's another magical phrase we invented to ridicule the truth seekers!"

"Routing RFK through the kitchen at the Ambassador Hotel – he wasn't supposed to go that way, you know – was like Dallas Mayor Cabell routing JFK through Dealey Plaza – you had conspirators in front and back – no way he's getting out of there alive!"

"Then we had to order the LA police to destroy the pictures that college student took – he documented Sirhan's position in the kitchen – never closer than five feet in front of RFK because of Roosevelt Grier and that steam table. I've seen those pictures – the second shooter – the security guard, Thane Eugene Cesar – was also photographed – that's why RFK grabbed his tie!"

"The pathologist, Dr. Noguchi, determined that all three RFK shots were contact shots from the rear! The security guard behind RFK first denied, then admitted that he fired his .22 caliber gun – the LA police arrested the decoy shooter, Sirhan Sirhan – who couldn't hit the broad side of a barn!"

"Attorney William Pepper noted that the acoustic tape analysis indicated 13 shots were fired, two of them being double shots – too close together to be fired by a single gun. Yet Sirhan's Iver-Johnson Cadet .22 caliber revolver held only eight shots!"

"That Special Unit Senator that was set up to investigate the RFK assassination used police officers that were active CIA operatives –

what a joke! Giancana reported that Sirhan, a horse trainer, was known to the Mafia and had gambling debts that he couldn't repay – he even played the street lottery on his way to the assassination!"

"Sirhan's lawyer, Grant Cooper, was also Johnny Roselli's lawyer. Cooper persuaded Sirhan to plead guilty, so there would be no trial and no presentation of evidence!"

"RFK Jr. has pleaded for his father's murder case to be reopened, but to no avail."

"No, Mr. President, we're not being run like a third world country – we control our cover-ups much better than a third world country!"

"You know, Mr. President, each country is like a Ship of State. And it's up to the intelligence community to guide that ship of state – Presidents come and go – it's up to the intelligence community – we're talking career experts here – to guide that Ship of State and keep it out of rough waters!"

"That's not a democracy, you say? True enough. Democracies are a fantasy, Mr. President. The dirty little secret is that the people don't always know best. Look no further than the rise of Adolph Hitler – a man adored by his people!"

"No, I like to consider the intelligence community as the puppet masters – we let the people think they're in control – we just pull the strings. And if you know what's best, Mr. President, you'll let us pull the strings! Got the picture?"

"My idea of the perfect President is a senile old man – we would control everything! All he'd have to do is read his que cards – we would control all the questions and we'd write all the answers! We'd control all the journalists, all the professors, all the corporate elites and all the social media tycoons!"

"Our main job would be to keep the President from misreading his teleprompter, or stumbling on camera as he climbed up the stairs of Air Force One! But enough of my fantasies!"

"Now, the CIA gets a little paranoid – John Jr. has also been doing some research on his father's assassination in 1963 – after all, the JFK assassination was a major trauma in his life at the age of three. One article in his *George* magazine was an Oliver Stone article entitled, *'Our Counterfeit History!'* Another article discussed the assassination of Yitzhak Rabin in Israel. Each country, Mr. President, has its' own skeletons in the closet – it's best not to rattle them!"

"Now, as the CIA sees it, the truth about the JFK assassination is something that must never be revealed – it would undermine the people's trust in their government, for God's sake! LBJ confides to his mistress, Madelaine Brown, that the CIA, the Texas oilmen, and the Mafia were all involved! Each country has its own red button – a secret set of histories they'd rather not share – you push that red button and, look out!"

"That Oliver Stone film, JFK, is the closest the people will ever come to knowing the truth, and even that should never have been released! We're still mad at Dr. Cyril Wecht for disputing the Warren Commission findings!"

"Every once in a while, the truth slips out – but there're so many false reports that nobody can tell the difference – that's the beauty of it all!"

"Now, you take Clint Hill – he's the Secret Service agent in Dealey Plaza who jumps off the running board of the trailing limo when the first shots are fired. He's running behind the Presidential limousine when he gets blasted with blood and brains from the head shot to JFK from the Grassy Knoll in front. He initially states the back of the head was gone! Then, forty years later, he changes his story and claims the shot came from behind. What a patriot!"

"And then there's the 1978 re-investigation by the House Select Intelligence Committee. They admit there was a Grassy Knoll shot, but in order to avoid the word 'conspiracy', they suggest that there may have been two independent shooters, one from the rear and one from the Grassy Knoll – both unaware of each other!"

"No, Mr. President, with regard to JFK, Jr., the CIA would not act alone in something like this – they would still have to get Presidential approval to make sure that a proper investigation was compromised. Many times, the cover-up is more important than the assassination itself!"

"JFK Jr.'s original plan was to fly alone – that was perfect. But at the last minute, his wife and sister-in-law decided to attend the wedding. The perpetrators had to call again, and once again Presidential approval was granted."

"No, President Clinton would have nothing to gain – after all, he was already President!"

"Yes, Clinton had close ties with the CIA with all those Mena, Arkansas drug running shenanigans, when he was governor of Arkansas. In fact, the CIA brags about helping Clinton become President – they covered up for him and all his peccadillos!"

"You're asking about Hillary? No, never! Rivals within the Democratic party would never think about killing each other! I don't think this was discussed with Hillary, and, if it was, she would never give approval for the murder of her political rival in New York, for God's sake! Let's be reasonable here!"

"We had JFK Jr. under surveillance – he knew his phones were tapped—he didn't like Hillary from Chicago 'insinuating' herself in New York as he put it. He had his eye on that Senate seat in New York, just like Hillary, who was starting her political career. And he knows he could beat her!"

"We warned him to stay out of politics, but he wouldn't listen – it's not our fault!"

"But it wasn't the Clintons who got the ball rolling – it was the CIA who cooked this up. All the President had to do was give it the nod. The Bushes, with all their CIA involvement, were very interested in protecting the CIA, so senior members of both political parties had to give it the nod. Let's just call it a collective decision. The only one they left out was Mr. Righteous – Jimmy Carter!"

"Preposterous, you say, Mr. President? These plans came from the same group that gave you Operation Northwoods – a plan by the CIA in the sixties to blow up an astronaut on the launch pad and blame it on Fidel Castro! JFK had to turn it down, or they would have proceeded! Did you know that John Jr. actually met with Fidel Castro on his little island in 1997 – that sounded like treason to us! The FBI kept a phone tap on him after that!"

"On the other hand, Bill Clinton might not have known – he gave the most heartwarming tribute, with his voice breaking and tears in his eyes over the death of his wife's political rival. If that wasn't genuine, then he must be an uncommonly good liar!"

"Yes, Mr. President, that sounds like a good conspiracy theory. That whole notion of calling something a conspiracy theory was conceived by our own 'Operation Ridicule'-it lets us get away with murder!"

"The details? Mr. President, you don't need to know the details. The details are the nuts and bolts of what we do, what we're most proud of – it's kind of like a magic act – making a carefully planned sequence of events look like coincidence to a trusting public. In a sense, we create the public's reality by bestowing a pompous authority to blatant lies!"

"Alright, alright. It's not a magic act if you have to suppress witness reports. But I'll have to swear you to secrecy-well, never mind. You try to explain this to somebody, and they'll laugh in your face – that's the beauty of it! Besides, you don't want to cross the Intel Boys – they've got six ways to Sunday to take you down, Mr. President!"

"You want to know the details? Well, the key to understanding the JFK Jr. assassination is to listen to the witnesses – whose reports were published in the local newspapers that first day, then suppressed by investigators!"

"The first set of witnesses were in the control tower at Martha's Vineyard. JFK Jr. radioed the control tower at 9:39 pm, informed them he was on his final approach, and that he was landing to drop off his sister-in-law, and then proceed to Hyannis Port to attend a wedding."

"The second set of witnesses were on Philbin beach near Martha's Vineyard – the plane was only six minutes from landing, and it was a clear night in July. The witnesses reported hearing an explosion over the water one minute after the control tower conversation, accompanied by a flash of light in the sky at 9:40 pm."

"No, Mr. President a bomb detonated by pressure change is a possibility, but it's not precise enough. It was important for the plane to go down over water, and since JFK Jr. flew along the coast, only the last 30 miles or so was over water. If he had dropped down below the weather while over land, the bomb might have gone off too soon!"

"You see, with the plane in the water near Martha's Vineyard, the recovery could be controlled by the federal government, and things like a charred wreckage or evidence of a bomb blast could be covered up! The kid had the presence of mind to turn off the fuel switch, which tells me the bomb must have set the engine on fire. Initial reports indicated that printed circuits had melted. The widely scattered luggage and plane parts indicate an aerial explosion. The distress beacon floated all the way to Long Island! The Pentagon took over all communications – yet this was a civilian death – go figure. And that nine-month investigation by the FAA was laughable – like I say, we controlled everything!"

"The bomb went off only one minute after the radio communication, at 9:40 pm, which tells me that the assassin was monitoring the control tower communications near No Mans Island near Squibnocket and Montauk to let him know when to transmit the radio signal to detonate the bomb on the airplane."

"A speedboat was seen in the neighborhood of the explosion, which tells me that the perpetrators were probably sitting in the water under the flight path when they set off the bomb. Then they sped over to where the plane entered the water, just to make sure no survivors pop up out of the water, and off they go!"

"There's an 'accidental' six-hour delay in sending rescue boats, which gives the perpetrators plenty of time to get away! And with the water temperature at 68 degrees, any survivors would have died in four hours from hypothermia! Don't think they didn't have this all figured out!"

"This same method is used in the Middle East to plant a remote-control bomb in a terrorist's car or even a telephone – only when the terrorist is actually seen in the car or heard on the phone is the bomb detonated. These people take pride in their work – no mistakes – and no survivors!"

"The most important information – the last five minutes of conversation – was recorded on a solid-state chip – housed in a box that was designed to withstand a crash. The Intel boys actually listened to that conversation, as John struggled to fly the damaged plane, before destroying the chip!"

"That's very good, Mr. President. There is a historic parallel to the death of JFK's brother, Joseph Kennedy Jr., in August, 1944 over Blythburgh, East Suffolk England. Joseph, Jr. was a potential presidential candidate whose father's isolationism and early support for pre-war Germany had fallen into political disfavor with the hard liners, including Allen Dulles's Intel boys. FDR was addled and out of the loop by that time!"

Joseph Kennedy, Jr. was getting ready to jump out of a special bomber that was programmed to fly into a French bunker during World War II when an 'aberrant radio signal' set off the bomb over East Suffolk, England, fifteen minutes after takeoff, killing Joseph Kennedy Jr. – Joseph Kennedy Sr. blamed his earlier isolationist policies and his fallout with FDR's Brain Trust for his son's death!"

"The problem with the official story is that this was a remote-controlled bomber, not a remote-controlled bomb. You see, the bomb on Joseph Kennedy's plane was designed to go off on impact, not from an 'aberrant radio signal!'"

"Coincidence with JFK Jr.? Perhaps, you know intelligence agencies get off on that kind of stuff!"

"There you have it, Mr. President. The rest involved the cover-up. The federal government controlled everything in the JFK Jr. investigation!"

"Throw in a false radar report that was miraculously discovered days later, a false report of bad weather at Martha's Vineyard, and witness reports from the control tower and at the beach that were ignored, despite published observations in the local newspaper that the weather was clear, and the cover-up was complete!"

"John Kennedy Jr. was portrayed as an inadequately trained pilot who sustained spatial disorientation, who took off in bad weather, in a plane he was not familiar with. Nothing to see here, as they say!"

"We warned John Jr. to back off-all the kid had to do was forget about his father's assassination, and he could have joined the club – just like Huey Long's brother. But, no, he couldn't do that. He goes like Don Quixote on some unquenchable search for truth. Suffice it to say we warned him – but, no, he had to go and hang out with Oliver Stone and all those conspiracy buffs!"

"Just like his Dad, John Kennedy, who hung out with the Navy's James Forrestal, co-founder of the Majestic 12, and pushed for full UFO disclosure – we taught them both a lesson!"

"The JFK Jr assassination was a long time in the making – we had to wait for Jackie to pass – just like Octavian waited for Cleopatra to pass before they killed her son, Caesarion. We warned him plenty – it wasn't our fault – the kid asked for it. Don't mess where you shouldn't be a'messin!"

"Ghosts, Mr. President? Well, if there is life after death, I'm sure the ghost of Jacqueline Kennedy would be quite angry over her husband, John, her son, John Jr., and two brothers-in-law, Robert Kennedy and Joe Kennedy, Jr. all being killed by the Intel boys! They call it the Kennedy curse, but these weren't chance events – all these assassinations required intimate planning!"

"Does Jacqueline's ghost haunt the assassins? Perhaps, but if Jacqueline wished for anything, she would want the full truth revealed, and the Deep State machinations to be fully disclosed to an unsuspecting public that's been programmed to tune out whenever they hear the phrase, 'Conspiracy Theory'!"

"We all felt sorry when we heard that Jackie suffered for years from PTSD – that Grassy Knoll shooter used a mercury filled exploding bullet for the head shot – what a mess!"

"You think they should name an airport or football stadium for John Kennedy, Jr., Mr. President? How's that?"

"A tribute to all those in their prime who died tragically with unfulfilled expectations?"

"Perhaps so. But we can't let anyone undermine the public's trust in their government – it's all for the Greater Good, Mr. President. Just do what you're told, and we'll make you feel important, so you can get re-elected!"

"No, Mr. President. We can still learn from our mistakes – but the most important thing about making a mistake is to cover it up – that's how you maintain the people's confidence!"

"What's that, Mr. President? You want to tell the truth to the public? Well, go right ahead – you'll be promoting yet another conspiracy theory – you'll be laughed out of office!"

"Why do you think this country is so great? It's because we've been steering it in the right direction! Besides, if you spill all the dirt about our history, you'll have to rename all the streets and landmarks in town!"

"We are the true Masters of the Universe!"

"These explanations, Mr. President, are not intended for the General Public-we must protect our assets, you know!"

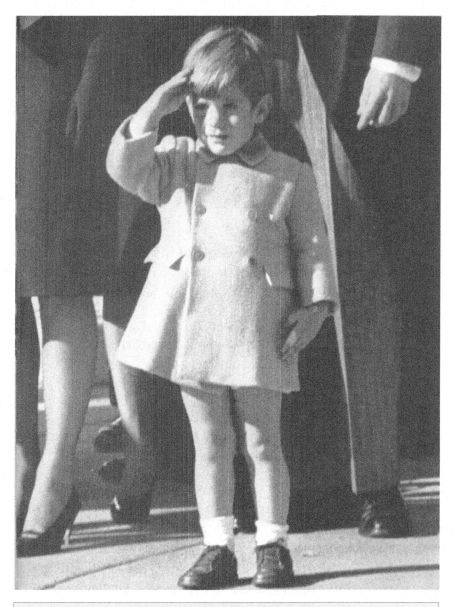

Photo of JFK Jr. by UPI photographer Stan Stearns

The People wondered,
"Who were the perpetrators of this loathsome Deed?"
But no one dared tell the People!
So, the Council decided, rather than share the Truth,
To let the People live their Delusion!
Thus, did the Myth endure!

THE AMELIA EARHART MYSTERY AND THE PEARL HARBOR "SURPRISE" ATTACK

"Now, I generally don't like to talk about the Pearl Harbor 'surprise' attack, Mr. President, but it's important for you to understand that sometimes it's necessary to manipulate the public for the Greater Good!"

"Yes, Mr. President we all cherish the democracy, but sometimes democracies sail off in the wrong direction, and it's necessary to make a correction from time to time for the Ship of State!"

"Now, don't be disillusioned, Mr. President – we all love a democracy, and that's important to sell to the public – I like to call these things course corrections!"

"You see, after World War I., which was supposed to make the world safe for democracy, according to Woodrow Wilson, there was no great desire to go to war against Germany in 1941. Our Intel boys in the OSS, like 'Wild Bill' Donovan and Allen Dulles, had been following the rise of Adolph Hitler and it didn't look good, especially after he annexed the Sudetenland in 1938 and then invaded Poland in 1939!"

"Despite all this, over 70% of Americans, in some polls as high as 90%, were opposed to going to war in Europe. Something had to be done to change American sentiments!"

"Now, the Japanese empire was also expanding, and Japan was quite anxious to keep us out of the Pacific. When Amelia Earhart's plane went down in the Pacific on July 2, 1937 – yes, she was captured by the Japanese along with her navigator, Fred Noonan – the Japanese privately offered a deal through France to release her, if we would stay out of the Pacific."

"The Japanese claimed Amelia was a spy – they couldn't believe all those rescue ships in the Pacific were for one aviator! They wanted the US to promise to stay out of the Pacific! FDR said 'no deal' and that was that. Her Macy's receipt and passport were recovered years later by a sailor in a safe on Saipan, but that was all kept quiet!"

"You see, James Forrestal played a role here. He proposed letting the Japanese keep their emperor – the Japanese then agreed to surrender, which avoided dropping the third atomic bomb. Then, in the further interest of peace, Forrestal suggested squelching the Amelia Earhart story, and both sides agreed! But Forrestal had other reasons to squelch Amelia's story – and burn her plane, with those two state-of-the-art Fairchild wing cameras!"

"It remains a secret, Mr. President, because it's embarrassing, and we don't reveal embarrassing stuff! In fact, we're still pressuring the Japanese government to keep it quiet! That damned History Channel spilled the beans on Amelia in 2017 – just like they did with Nigel Turner Productions on JFK in 1988. We've spent millions of dollars trying to discredit the truth and protect our assets!"

"We know Amelia and Fred landed on an island, because 57 radio messages were documented during the next five days. Gardner Island was overflown by planes from the Colorado on the second day. We know they landed on a beach, because the radio communications stopped during high tide, when they couldn't run the generator for the radio. But no plane was seen on the beach of this tiny island, so that rules out Gardner Island."

"The Gilbert Islands were under British control in 1937. The British would have jubilantly announced Amelia's arrival, so that rules out the Gilbert Islands. That leaves the Marshall Islands, which were part of the Japanese Mandate from the League of Nations in 1922."

"That two week multi-million-dollar naval search ordered by FDR thru July 18 was a ruse to convince the Japanese we didn't have their code!"

"The fact that there were secret negotiations with the Japanese in France tells you two things – Amelia and Fred were alive, and they landed in Japanese controlled territory – specifically, the Marshall Islands!"

"You're asking which Marshall Island, Mr. President? Numerous witnesses on the Mili Atoll in the Marshall Islands reported seeing Amelia and Fred, whose leg was injured in the crash landing. The plane, with a broken wing, was mounted on a cart and hauled across the island on a makeshift trolley from the ocean side to the deeper lagoon side and loaded on the back of the ship – named the *Koshu Maru*."

"Amelia and Fred were also placed aboard the *Koshu Maru*, and taken to Kwajalein Atoll and then Saipan. The ship stopped briefly at Jaluit, where Amelia is seen from behind, while sitting on the dock, with the plane mounted on the rear of the ship! The Intel agencies have done their best to discredit that photo – they claim the photo was taken in 1935, but that dock wasn't upgraded until 1936!"

"Both Amelia and Fred were treated as spies by the Japanese. When negotiations failed, they died in Japanese custody. Amelia and Fred were held in Garapan prison on Saipan and were killed on direct orders from General Tojo in Tokyo, who would later hang for his war crimes. Their bodies were later dug up and moved from a Catholic cemetery by the U.S. Intel services."

"Look, Mr. President. I'm not proud of how we handled it. Neither are the Japanese. Let's just let bygones be bygones! We're just too embarrassed to tell the whole truth, and we've got to protect our assets!"

"You want the whole truth, Mr. President? Well, it's not very pretty. Look, the American government was paying indirectly for a lot of Amelia's 'round the world trip. The Intel boys just wanted a little something in return. You know, we didn't have satellites in those days and we wanted to know what the Japanese were up to! FDR and Eleanor talked to her and indirectly footed the bill."

"The island of Truk was under Japanese control and had a natural harbor for the Imperial Navy's largest ships. The Intel Boys were really anxious to have a look. It was just a little north of Amelia's flight path from Lae in New Guinea to Howland Island."

"We were quite concerned about Japan's illegal buildup of military infrastructure in the Marshall Islands – FDR had plans to take Japan to what became the World Court in the Netherlands – but we needed photographic evidence! The plan was to stop the Japanese westward expansion in hopes of avoiding a war that would cost thousands of American lives! Was that so terrible?"

"Amelia's Electra E-10 was modified by Kelly Johnson of Skunk Works fame and various versions were later used for spy activity around the world. Kelly's idea for a spy plane was to fly higher and faster than the competition – just like the later U-2 and the SR-71!"

"With a normal fuel load of 200 gallons, the plane could fly 800 miles – that's four miles to the gallon. But with extra fuselage tanks that carried a total of 1,150 gallons of fuel, weighing an extra three tons, the range was extended to 4,000 miles. This required the plane to be souped up with much larger high tech 600 hp supercharged engines, which were known for their temperamental nature and tendency to overheat! The pressurized plane had a service ceiling of 30,000 feet!"

"That crash in Hawaii before the world flight was a ruse to get Amelia a whole new plane from Lockheed with all the latest gadgets! They even transferred the old tail numbers to the new plane, courtesy of Uncle Sam! Kelly's idea for a spy plane was to fly higher and faster than everybody else! They took out the large side windows and pressurized the entire cabin using the engine supercharger compressors! They did the same thing to the Lockheed Electra XC-35 one month later."

"We had two of the latest Fairchild surveillance cameras fitted on her wings by Lockheed in Burbank – she could photograph at 30,000 feet without oxygen and avoid detection! But we had trouble with them in New Guinea-that's why she was two days late getting started – the damned things wouldn't work – so they blamed poor Fred's drinking for the late start!"

"The plan was for Amelia to claim she got lost or re-directed by the weather on her around the world trip. She would secretly gather photographic intel over the Marshall Islands, then land at Howland Island! You know, the government still classifies her flight plan!"

"You want more details, Mr. President? Well, the trip to Howland Island was 2,500 miles – but they could fly at least 3,500 miles at 160 mph! Secondly, Major Earhart was a commissioned officer in the Army Air Force Reserves – a true patriot. Her dangerous overflight of the Marshall Islands was sanctioned by FDR and the Intel Boys and the plane was specially fitted by the future Skunk Works team at Lockheed – Amelia called it her laboratory!"

"The high-flying pressurized Lockheed Electra 10-E flew higher than the Japanese open cockpit ASM-5 fighters in 1937, so I don't believe they were shot down. Also, it wouldn't have taken a week for the Japanese to find Amelia and Fred if they had been shot down!"

"So, Amelia and Fred head a little north of the purported flight plan, and take a few pics over Truk Island and some of the Marshall Islands. But there's a 25-mph wind that blows them northeast. After 20 hours of flying, they're still 800 miles from Howland Island and they're running out of gas!"

"The port engine was leaking fuel and caught on fire, just like on Amelia's trial flight in Tucson a month earlier on May 22. Amelia was forced to land on the coral reef on Endriken Island at the Mili Atoll in the Marshall Islands. Amelia sustained burns to her left arm, hand, and body, according to witnesses at the local hospital and subsequently at Garapan prison."

"Fred, stationed in the back of the plane, sustained a leg wound during the crash landing. And what an amazing landing! We picked up their voice and Morse code messages in New Zealand and on the Lexington aircraft carrier, so we knew they were down!"

"They lived on clams and crabs for seven days, transmitting daily. Using his sextant, Fred radioed a star fix to the Lexington. But our Navy cancelled a rescue plan to the Marshall Islands, which made Fred furious – he starts yelling into the microphone! The Japanese sent a cable on July 5, advising the U.S. not to enter the Marshall Islands while the Japanese were looking for Amelia and Fred among the 29 Atolls and five islands using direction finder equipment!"

"You know, over 200 natives saw or heard of Amelia on the Mili Atoll and Saipan – a white female pilot on a small Asian island with short hair, wearing long pants and boots, made quite a sensation! We solved that problem by calling it a mass hallucination, limited to those two islands!"

"Despite the secrecy surrounding Amelia, her presence in Saipan at the Garapan prison was common knowledge among the Chamorro natives!"

"To the natives on Saipan, Amelia was a God-like figure who descended from the heavens – a lanky female pilot with short hair and high boots, who captured the imagination not only of the American women but of the Chamorro women as well! The little island would eventually issue commemorative stamps in 1987 with Amelia and Fred standing next to their damaged plane on the coral reef!"

"When the Americans captured Saipan in June 1944, Amelia's presence on the island continued to be squelched – the United States cut a deal with Japan for both sides to bury the truth – stories of Amelia by hundreds of natives on two specific islands – the Mili Atoll and then Saipan – are now described as mass hallucinations!"

"I never thought of it that way, Mr. President, but it is a little condescending to simply deny the verbal accounts of hundreds of Chamorro natives on two remote islands, separated by 1,800 miles! Reliance on documents, which can be easily altered or shredded, is no more credible!"

"Look, Mr. President – neither side had anything to gain. From the American standpoint, why did the Intel boys put Amelia and Fred in harm's way? From the Japanese standpoint, why were the Japanese so cruel to Amelia and Fred – the US and Japan weren't even at war!"

"The solution was simple – both sides would deny that it ever happened! Simply declare that Fred was a bad navigator and Amelia was a bad pilot and they ran out of gas over the Pacific – end of story! That also saved FDR's back side for not approving a rather dangerous rescue mission!"

"No, Mr. President, I didn't say we were protecting our posterior – I said we were protecting our posterity! It's important for future generations of spies to honor our forefathers with positive memories!"

"Yes, Mr. President, this was very much a military mission. Amelia was a commissioned officer in the U.S. Army Air Force reserves! Someday, Major Earhart and Merchant Mariner Fred Noonan will be honored with a state funeral and a military flyover! There needs to be an award for heroism and patriotic feminism!"

"The Navy actually did a limited hangout in the movie, *Flight for Freedom*, in 1943 with Rosalind Russel playing an animated, groundbreaking female aviator who was recruited by the Navy Intel boys to take reconnaissance photos and document the Japanese military build-up over the Marshall Islands on the last leg of her around the world journey! The movie explains how surveillance photos of the Marshall Islands were crucial in determining which islands to bomb once the war started!"

"I've heard that the Japanese government is willing to put their cards on the table, but our Intel Boys are still pressuring them to remain silent!"

"Now, getting back to Pearl Harbor in December 1941-we had broken the Japanese code – Harry Stimson and the Intel boys even knew which ship Yamamoto was on – the Japanese would start each message with the name of the ship that was transmitting the message!"

"No, they didn't maintain radio silence – they were even picked up by ocean liners, who relayed that they were hearing chatter – even some of our listening stations in California were picking them up – the Japanese hadn't yet learned about 'bounce' transmissions off the ionosphere!"

"We also knew that Yamamoto had given orders not to attack if the Americans had spotted them before the planes arrived – it had to be a surprise attack. So, our top echelon had orders – don't sound the general alarm until the first bomb drops!"

"The first general quarters battle stations alarm was not sounded until the first Japanese Zero's torpedoes had exploded! But one Japanese minisub had already been spotted, then fired upon and sunk by the U.S.S. Ward an hour earlier by American sailors, who were then sworn to secrecy under threat of death!"

"Another small plane had taken off and dropped a depth charge on another minisub, but general quarters was still not sounded! And the radar operator reported that the planes approaching on his radar scope were not American planes, but this was also ignored!"

"Three American aircraft carriers had set sail the night before – just another coincidence, you know – sailing away in the opposite direction from the Japanese. Yamamoto was so concerned about the missing American aircraft carriers, which were his prime target, that he suspected a counterattack. He cancelled the second wave of fighters – to the extreme dismay of his returning fighter pilots-fearing a surprise counterattack from the American carriers!"

"We all felt bad about those 429 sailors trapped aboard the USS Oklahoma after she capsized, as well as the 1,177 men killed aboard the USS Arizona when she exploded and sank. If they had sounded general quarters an hour earlier, those men would have been topside, but Admiral Yamamoto might have called off the attack, for God's sake!"

"I know this whole thing sounds cruel, Mr. President, but American opinion changed overnight, and American involvement in World War II. had finally begun! Those brave sailors at Pearl Harbor saved the world from the evils of Nazism – it was all for the Greater Good! How else was Germany to be defeated without American involvement in World War II.?"

"Now, Mr. President, the reason I'm telling this story – the message for you here – is that sometimes you've got to deliberately fool the public! The idea is to alter the public perception of events in order to shape government policy!"

Remember, this is one of our country's greatest secrets – any attempt by you to spill the beans and to come clean and tell the truth, and we'll clean your clock! Kapische?"

"This explanation, Mr. President, is not intended for the General Public – it's important to protect our assets!"

Thus, did the King suffer in Silence –
For nobody dared reveal his Limitations!
And, though they trusted him once –
They trusted him no more!
How quickly the Hunters become the Hunted!

FRANKLIN DELANO ROOSEVELT

"Do you want to know about FDR's demise, Mr. President?"

"You already know? Yes, well, FDR died of a cerebral hemorrhage, alright – but it was from a .38 caliber bullet!"

"You don't believe me? Well, fair enough – we'll go to JFK and skip FDR."

"Yes, FDR was our greatest President during times of turmoil – the Depression and the second World War."

"I thought you didn't want to hear about it, Mr. President."

"Well, O.K. Let me start from the beginning. FDR gets what they called an unusual form of polio at the age of 39 in 1921 and becomes paralyzed, but still manages to become President in 1933 – quite an accomplishment!"

"FDR was what you call a 'cad' or roundabout, like most politicians, during an era when social diseases had few cures – penicillin didn't make it until 1942. Some of the rumors included a positive VDRL test after Dr. Frank Lahey and a group of doctors were commissioned to evaluate FDR's declining health status in March, 1944. Dr. Lahey was an honest man – a straight shooter who was quite upset about FDR's mental capacity, severe headaches, tremors, confabulation, and black-out episodes – symptoms compatible with neurosyphilis that were labeled 'post-polio syndrome.'"

"Also, coincidentally in March, 1944, 39-year-old Dr. Howard Bruenn was hired to be FDR's personal cardiologist, and to accompany the President on his trips to the Little White House in Warm Springs, Georgia."

"Dr. Lahey wrote a confidential note, warning that FDR would die in office if he ran for reelection, and he privately discussed these results with other physicians at surgical meetings, like Dr. Neil Woodward in Oklahoma City. I personally worked with his son, Dr. Neil Woodward, Jr. for over 20 years. In fact, Roosevelt's last State of the Union address was pre-recorded! But who knows for sure – his health records were all gathered and put into a vault at the Bethesda Hospital – where they disappeared three weeks after his death!"

"FDR originally calls himself a pacifist, but plots with Churchill about getting American involvement in World War II. After the 'surprise' attack on Pearl Harbor by Japan, the nation rightfully endorses the war against Germany. We become a close ally with Russia against Germany, and FDR and Stalin become good friends—too good for the Intel boys, who see Russia as an eventual Cold War threat!"

"Now, Allen Dulles is in Bern, Switzerland, in March, 1945, trying to negotiate with the Germans for an early surrender in Italy – Operation Sunrise they called it. Stalin wants to be included in any negotiations, and FDR on March 25 wants Dulles to include the Russians in any negotiations."

"This infuriates Dulles, who does not want to include the Russians in any discussions. There are even plans, sponsored by Winston Churchill (Operation Unthinkable) to have the English and Americans sign a separate peace accord with Germany, then have the Germans in northern Italy counterattack against the Russians!"

"But something had to be done about FDR and his Brain Trust – you can't have the President getting in the way of the Intel Chief! FDR's sudden death two weeks later, on April 12, 1945, occurred during the heat of these discussions! Nevertheless, the official German surrender in Italy occurred on April 29, 1945, and included all parties."

"FDR had been in poor health with severe headaches and total body pain, which they're calling post-polio syndrome – Presidents don't get neurosyphilis! The Intel boys feel that FDR is 'non compos mentis' at this time, especially with his giveaways to Stalin at the Yalta conference!"

FDR was to meet with disadvantaged children on the afternoon of his death

"Enter Dr. Howard Bruenn – a young, 39-year-old unsuspecting cardiologist who, in March, 1944 is assigned by Dr Ross McIntire, to stay with FDR, including his visits to his Warm Springs compound, the Little White House."

"Why is that important? Well, the usual situation if a President has a 'cerebral bleed' is to take him to the hospital--in Warm Springs, that's only five minutes away. But that allows a lot more witnesses to observe the President – if there's any hanky-panky, it's a lot harder to cover it up! With a doctor in residence at the Little White House in Warm Springs, there's no need to go to the hospital!"

"So, after FDR collapses, Dr. Bruenn calls Dr. McIntire in Washington and is ordered to keep FDR at the Warm Springs compound on April 12, 1945 – the official story is that FDR's brain bleed is so bad that there's no point in going to the hospital – especially with Dr. Bruenn present at the Little White House!"

"Can you believe that? The President of the United States is reported to suffer a massive stroke, and the official story is that there's no point in taking him to the hospital, which is five minutes away!"

"As was his custom, FDR had gone off in his wheelchair to eat breakfast in his pajamas, to a secluded, peaceful area at the Warm Springs compound. There are hints about what really happened – Eleanor Roosevelt says her husband 'died like a soldier,' and witnesses relate that FDR was a 'dead weight' when they transferred him to his bed!"

"Daisy Suckley complained that there was no security to be found around the President at the time of his mishap – but how would security help a person who just had a stroke – if that's what FDR really had?"

"They cooked up a cover story that FDR was sitting for a painting, like he had the two previous days, by Elizabeth Shoumatoff, a Russian émigré artist. Purportedly re-dressed in his three-piece suit, FDR exclaimed, 'I have a terrible headache' and then collapsed. Then they supposedly changed this unconscious, 190 pound man back into his pajamas and put him in bed!"

"How do I know it was a .38 caliber bullet if no x-rays were taken? Good question, Mr. President."

"There was a .38 caliber Derringer next to his wheelchair – similar to Lincoln – the Intel boys get off on that kind of stuff! After the war, Dr. Bruenn, an honest man who was troubled by the cover-up, confides in a letter to one of his former naval colleagues, Dr. Harlan Sowell in Oklahoma City, that FDR died from a cerebral hemorrhage alright-from a .38 caliber bullet!"

"I personally talked to two doctors who I worked with for over ten years – Dr. Karl Boatman, chief of surgery at Baptist Hospital, who was on a hunting trip with his anesthesiologist, Dr. Harlan Sowell, when the letter was discussed, and Dr. Sowell's son, Dr. Doug Sowell DPM, president of the American Podiatry Association, who both independently confirmed this letter."

"I offered to purchase or at least photograph this letter from Dr. Doug Sowell, who was quite surprised, even shocked, that I knew about this letter. Several days later, he guardedly told me that he could not find the letter."

"The back-up story is that this was a suicide, but Eleanor knew better – there was an afternoon minstrel show with the disadvantaged kids that Franklin always liked to attend. That's why she said that FDR died like a soldier – she knew someone had shot him!"

"That's right, Mr. President – FDR was right-handed, but the swelling occurred on the left side of the head and neck!"

"Eleanor insists upon a closed casket, refuses an autopsy, and does not allow her son, Elliott, to return from the Pacific. She opens the casket only after ordering everyone to leave the rotunda. The undertaker relates that there was an 'embalming error' which caused the left side of the head to swell and turn purple – the same thing that happens with a gunshot wound! Eleanor also complained about the embalming error, which she stated was the reason for the closed casket!"

"J. Edgar Hoover sends the FBI into Warm Springs to silence the witnesses – case closed!"

"You ask me why Eleanor didn't blow the whistle? Maybe, with the US at war, this would have been demoralizing – especially with the stigma of a potential suicide explanation- or a positive VDRL test for syphilis!"

"The important lesson for you, Mr. President, is that FDR wasn't following what the Intel boys were trying to do in Europe – he was too close to Joseph Stalin!"

"And his trusted aid and chief confidant, Harry Hopkins, leader of the 'Brain Trust' was busy sending yellow cake uranium, heavy water and aluminum tubes (which are used to convert uranium to plutonium) to Russia via the Lend Lease Act, which infuriated J. Edgar Hoover! The Russians later identified Hopkins as 'Agent 19' – they claimed he was the most important of all Soviet wartime agents!"

"Officially, Dulles' behavior is criticized for overruling President Roosevelt in an attempt to take charge and enhance the reputation of the newly formed Office of Strategic Services – the precursor to the CIA. But all Dulles was trying to do was to use the Germans to prevent Russia from grabbing more land!"

"The only problem with the Roosevelt assassination is that we should have done it earlier – before the Yalta conference in February – when FDR gave away the Eastern Bloc to Stalin!"

"I guess you could say, Mr. President, that FDR was the first victim of the impending Cold War with Russia!"

"You find this all hard to believe, Mr. President? Well, the best is yet to come!"

"This explanation, Mr. President, is not intended for the General Public – we've got to protect our assets!"

FDR at Yalta

With his Queen at his side,
King John was struck down by the Lightning of the Corrupters!
And the King's Chariot did fill with blood!
For thus spoke the Jester, "If you strike the King, you must kill Him!"

And the People grieved mightily, for great was the Tragedy thereof!
And Robert Groden, the Watchman,
for Fifty Years keeps his lonely Dealey Plaza Vigil —
Lecturing Visitors, from around the World –
Who listen in Awe and take Pictures-Hoping to capture the Past!

THE JFK ASSASSINATION

"O.K, O.K. – you want to hear about John Kennedy. The JFK assassination is kind of a sticky wicket. Officially, we've been telling our boys that it was a job well done, but truth be known, it remains one of our darkest secrets – we're still generating disinformation fifty years later!"

"After the Bay of Pigs fiasco, where JFK refused to let our troop carriers land – they were sitting offshore from Cuba, for God's sake, then the Berlin Wall fiasco where JFK caved into the Russians, and then his indecision over sending more troops to Viet Nam, the Intel boys just had all they could take. You can learn all this by watching Oliver Stone's movie, 'JFK' – how he got that produced, I'll never know – we gave it all the bad publicity we could muster!"

"Add to this, the Cuban Missile Crisis, where we almost had a nuclear war, and where the Cuban missiles were never truly removed, Allen Dulles and the Intel boys had all they could take!"

"You know, we were dropping depth charges around this Russian submarine with nuclear missiles as part of the naval blockade during the Cuban Missile Crisis. The Russian commander had no way of knowing if a war had begun, and we had no way of knowing this was a nuclear missile submarine!"

"So – most people don't know this – the Russian submarine commander actually fired a nuclear tipped missile! Now, these missiles are vulnerable for a few seconds after they pop out of the water on compressed air – before the rocket motor fires. We actually fired at this missile just as it exited the water and destroyed it!"

"What if the missile had gotten away, you wonder? I don't know – probably a nuclear war, where Russia and the U.S. destroy each other! Maybe the space aliens would have stepped in and shot it down!"

"Yes, aliens exist, Mr. President – we'll get to that later!"

"Another thing most people don't know – we had Navy seals, dressed as civilians, leave with the Guantanamo daily civilian bus and sneak onto the missile sites and re-program the Cuban missiles to fall to a harmless location – courtesy of the Russians – and unbeknownst to Castro! We also disabled the nuclear firing pins on those weapons! That's a Seal mission that will never be disclosed!"

"Do you know, Mr. President, that Fidel Castro was actually goading Khrushchev into a first strike nuclear war? Castro was willing to have Cuba destroyed if it meant destroying the United States! Castro denied this until Khrushchev showed him the transcript years later during his visit to Russia. Castro's only response was that, 'Things at times were quite intense!'"

"And Che Guevara, that doctor turned rebel fighter, was pushing for a first strike nuclear attack against the United States – some hero!"

"But the crowning blow, the trigger point if you will, for the JFK assassination was JFK's desire for full disclosure of UFOs and sharing of information with the Russians! Kennedy even got Khrushchev to agree on a joint Russian-American moon mission!"

"As described by Michael Salla, Kennedy's mandate for disclosure occurred only weeks before his Dallas trip. This would have declassified the CIA's crown jewels – knowledge about antigravity, electrogravitic devices, and time travel that we had reverse engineered from crashed UFOs and re-patriated German scientists from World War II! We're talking about two trillion dollars in classified research projects that are outside the Federal budget!"

"Do you know, Mr. President, that an electrical charge can be used to decrease or even neutralize gravity – it's called the Brown-Biefeld effect – it's used in the B-2 bomber to lighten the plane, but they won't teach it in college physics!"

"JFK's knowledge about UFOs dates all the way back to July, 1945 with his close friendship with James Forrestal, the secretary of the Navy, who was a founding member of MJ-12. JFK actually accompanied Forrestal on his trips to post-war Germany. The 28-year-old JFK kept a daily diary which described the devastation along the Unter Den Linden boulevard in Berlin and his trip to Hitler's 'Eagle's Nest' lair in Berchtesgaden, Bavaria."

"JFK observed that the German Schnellboot E-boats were superior to his PT 109! Others have reported that Forrestal examined the four UFOs that were brought back to Area 51 after the war. Forrestal pushed for full UFO disclosure before he was suicided in 1949!"

"So, a JFK assassination plan was hatched in the spring of 1963 – it followed the Huey Long model with a patsy who never fired a shot, compromised security, compromised news media, and witness intimidation!"

"A Mafia-CIA teamed had already been formed to try to kill Fidel Castro using snipers – we also tried food poisoning, and even a contaminated diving suit, but Castro wouldn't take the bait!"

"The Mafia, Mr. President? Of course, they were involved – Giancana out of Chicago brought in two of the shooters – we farm things out, you know – we like to keep a professional distance."

"No, Mr. President – we're not the same as the Mafia. You see, the Mafia has no morals, but they have rules, whereas we in the intelligence agencies have morals, but no rules – it's a match made in heaven, don't you know! The idea is to maintain the people's trust, even if you have to temporarily lie!"

"How long do we lie? Oh, I don't know – fifty or a hundred years, maybe. Those JFK buffs are still trying to get those records released! But all they have to do is read Judyth Vary Baker's book! Can you imagine that Oswald's scientist-girlfriend, a gifted honor student who worked for Dr. Ochsner in New Orleans, resurfaces in 2011 with a photographic memory for names and dates and totally exonerates Oswald! We worked hard to discredit her!"

"The CIA gave up Oswald – his main fault was being too naïve and trusting his superiors, though he had his suspicions. With his defection to Russia, which was part of a CIA spy program, and his orders to create a 'Fair Play for Cuba' committee, of which he was the only member, he was the perfect patsy! His girlfriend, Judyth Baker, relates Oswald's suspicions that he was being 'sheep dipped' as a communist sympathizer! Every once in a while, we have to give up one of our own!"

"Judyth Baker was a truth teller with a photographic memory for names and dates. She worked as a research scientist in David Ferrie's lab for Dr. Ochsner. She blew up the whole 'Oswald did it' scenario. We blocked her at every turn – she wasn't even allowed to speak at the JFK Lancer conspiracy meetings, held every year in Dallas!"

"You know, Oswald twice warned the FBI about JFK assassination plans – he had his own FBI informant number, after all. He phones the FBI in Chicago and helps head off the earlier Chicago assassination plans. Then he writes a note to FBI agent Hosty in Dallas, warning about the Dealey Plaza assassination plans. Hoover later orders Hosty to destroy the note!"

"Fast forward to Dealey Plaza in Dallas. Oswald is on the second floor of the Book Depository, and is not a shooter. Furthermore, a Depository oak tree blocks a clear view of the JFK motorcade during the first volley of shots – the Depository is a decoy position – any shooter knows this! Two shooters are in the Dal-Tex building, which provides a perfect straight-line view down Elm Street!"

"A dictabelt tape at the police station records five supersonic impulses, due to Officer McLain's open motorcycle microphone – three during the first volley, then a five second pause, then two shots very close together for the second volley."

"You're right, Mr. President. Some researchers don't believe the acoustics. But, tell me, what else is going to cause five supersonic oscilloscope chirps in Dealey Plaza, just as JFK rides through on his motorcade – squirrels?"

"The first shot creates sparks off the cement, as it sails a few inches over JFK's head, due to the downslope on Elm Street. Witnesses thought that the first sound was a firecracker thrown by a prankster, complete with sparks. The bullet travels over the windshield, and strikes Elm Street, causing sparks, then hits the curb in front of the innocent bystander, James Tague at the triple underpass. This shot traces back to the Dal-Tex building!"

"If you go to Dealey Plaza in Dallas, stand in front of the Depository and point your arm where James Tague was standing at the Triple Underpass, your arm, which traces the path of the bullet, will cross Elm Street at Zapruder frame 440 – but by now the assassination is over – it ended at Zapruder frame 330!"

"But if you stand in front of the Dal-Tex building and point your arm where James Tague was standing at the south end of the Triple Overpass, your arm crosses Elm Street during the first volley, where sparks were seen as the bullet hit Elm Street! This further confirms the Dal-Tex building as the point of origin for the rear shots – not the Depository!"

"The second shot strikes JFK in the extreme upper right shoulder at the lower edge of the shirt collar at C7, then nicks the transverse process of the T1 vertebrae, as seen on X-ray, then exits JFK's throat, just above the sternal notch."

"You say, Mr. President, that the wound in the throat is too small to be an exit wound? It was described to me by one of the Parkland surgeons, Dr. Crenshaw, as the size of a pencil – about 6 mm. Mr. President, you need to talk to some wounded war veterans – if a rifle bullet does not strike bone, it can be impossible to tell an entry wound from an exit wound. JFK's exit wound in the neck is small, because it's a jacketed bullet that never strikes any significant bone!"

"JFK says, 'I'm hit – get me to the hospital!' and grabs his throat!"

"Now, the third shot strikes Governor Connally, as by now he has turned to his right and looks back. The bullet enters near his right armpit and exits at the right nipple. Both JFK and Connally were hit with separate shots – there was no 'magic bullet' that went through both of them."

"Now, here's where it gets interesting. Driver Greer looks back, as seen on the Zapruder film, which they never should have released, and puts on the brakes, instead of following protocol and speeding up, as seen in the Muchmore film, where the brakes light up."

"Witness Bill Newman at the Grassy Knoll told me the car actually stopped before the head shot. This violates all protocol! JFK's confidante, David Powers, riding in the car behind JFK, feels like he's heading into an ambush as the car slows down – before he reports hearing the loud Grassy Knoll head shot!"

"That's right, Mr. President – the car is not seen to stop on the Zapruder film – the wonder of editing! Journalist Julian Read was watching from the journalist trailing bus when he described hearing three shots, then said the JFK limo almost stopped, as Jackie crawled onto the trunk to retrieve the skull, then lurched forward toward the underpass!"

"The acoustic tape also records a single carillon church bell ring right after the assassination, probably from a distant church at 12:30 pm – ask not for whom the bell tolls – it tolls for thee and me!"

"On the acoustic tape, there's a five second pause after the third shot. Then the fourth shot, the headshot, is fired from the Grassy Knoll to the right and in front of JFK. Acoustic echoes, just like the sonar on submarines, localize this shot to the corner of the picket fence at the Grassy Knoll!"

"Clint Hill, the Secret Service man, has jumped off the left side of the trailing car, and is running towards the JFK limo. As he crosses behind the presidential limo, he temporarily blocks a rear shot, which causes the five second delay between the two volleys. Then the head shot is fired from the Grassy Knoll to the front right, and Clint Hill gets hit with blood and brain tissue, as does the motorcycle policeman, Bobby Hargis, riding behind and to the left of JFK – he even has fragments of bone imbedded in his vest!"

"The motorcycle policemen, instead of riding even with the limo to provide protection, are ordered to ride behind the limo – another violation of protocol! Bill Newman and his family fall to the ground at the Grassy Knoll as the loud shot is fired from behind them from the Grassy Knoll. Mr. Newman, the closest witness to the assassination, is never called by the Warren Commission!"

"The fifth shot heard on the acoustics is fired only seven tenths of a second later from the rear and strikes the back of Connally's upraised wrist, causing him to drop his Stetson Hat! The last two shots are so close together that witnesses called it an echo!"

"When James Files, the Mafia-CIA shooter at the Grassy Knoll gets back to the getaway car, Charles Niccoletti, the Mafia-CIA shooter in the Dal-Tex, is mad at Files for firing too soon! Niccoletti maintains that his rear shot would have killed JFK, thus avoiding the shot from the Grassy Knoll!"

"Our Intel boys recreated Dealey Plaza using lasers and a computer – we concluded that Niccoletti was wrong – his final rear shot would have missed JFK high! Files maintained that, had he waited any longer, Jacqueline Kennedy would have been in his line of fire, and that he had strict orders not to hurt Jackie!"

"After that Bahia de Cochinos fiasco (Bay of Pigs), Kennedy threatened to break the CIA into a thousand pieces. Instead, we broke JFK into a thousand pieces! I mean the motorcycle policeman, riding behind and to the left of JFK, was hit with so much debris that he thought that he had been shot! That means the fatal shot had to come from ahead and to the right of JFK – from the Grassy Knoll!"

"I can tell you that the JFK assassination would have been much easier to cover up, but for that Grassy Knoll shot! That's really what forced LBJ to create the Warren Commission!"

"You ask if the Secret Service was involved? Mr. President, the Secret Service is sworn to protect the President with their own lives!"

"Alright, alright – researcher Vince Palamara uncovered too much and it's all public now. The Secret Service ordered their own agents off the back of the Kennedy limo at the Dallas airport – they've even got that on film! That was crucial for those rear shots. The Big Lie was that Kennedy ordered them off – but JFK never compromised his own security!"

"Also, Driver Greer slowed the car down in the middle of the assassination, instead of stepping on the gas – the brake lights are seen to come on in the Moorman film, as Driver Greer puts on the brakes and looks back."

"Kennedy has to yell at his own driver, 'I'm hit – get me to the hospital!' as he grabs his throat where the rear shot exited!"

"And don't forget the police – the motorcycle policemen had to be ordered by Mayor Earle Cabell, brother of the CIA's Charles Cabell, to ride behind the Kennedy limo, instead of their usual protective position side-by-side. That allowed the Grassy Knoll shooter to have a clear shot! The Mayor was also in charge of planning the motorcade route through Dealey Plaza with that hairpin turn and all those open windows!"

"That's right, Mr. President – it seems that everyone knew about the JFK assassination plans – the Russians, who tried to stop it, the Cubans who disapproved, the FBI from Oswald's note to Agent Hosty, the CIA and Mafia who planned it, the Secret Service, who ordered agents off the back of the limo, the Dallas Mayor who ordered the motorcycle escorts to stay back, Lyndon Johnson, who tried to get his political opponent Ralph Yarborough instead of Connally into the jump seat in front of the President, and who even ducked in the trailing car before shots were fired, and who told his mistress Madeleine Brown the night before – the only one who didn't know about it was JFK!"

"There's a physician, Dr. Bill Truels, who described the JFK assassination in his book, *Breach of Faith*, as a Grand Unified Theory – he proposed coordination among a large number of people and even agencies to make the JFK assassination look like a crazed, lone gunman – pure magic, I tell 'ya!"

"Corruption? Mr. President, I wouldn't call it corruption – it's important for Intel agencies to practice deception – that's the art of telling the truth while you're lying! When a magician performs a magic act, he's really practicing slight of hand – a form of deception. If it's done properly, people call it magic!"

"Mr. President, we're really all magicians, practicing our art. The JFK assassination involved dozens of people, all working together to create a perceived random act by a crazed lone gunman!"

"But there was a problem with the witnesses. James Files talks about how the jeweler who made the mercury filled bullets for the Grassy Knoll shot was killed only days after Files revealed his name!"

"James Files also talks about how David Ferrie was murdered before he could testify to Jim Garrison – this pathologist, with a high falutin medical degree, concludes that Ferrie died from a stroke due to high blood pressure."

"James Files, with an eighth-grade education, talks about forcing a metal nail file with corrugated edges up through the soft palate, through the cribriform plate and into the brain to tear a blood vessel, and fool the pathologist into thinking it was a stroke, only days before Ferrie was scheduled to testify for Jim Garrison!"

"Sometimes the most highly educated people are the easiest to fool – they've grown up in the system and learned to trust the establishment – they can't accept an alternate explanation! In fact, we're planning to arrest people for leaking the truth – it's high time we button things down a little! The predilection for certain reporters to tell the truth has simply got to stop!"

"Johnny Roselli testified before the Church Committee in 1975 and provided a limited hang-out. Roselli tried to blame Fidel Castro by saying that the Mafia-CIA shooters had been sent to Cuba but were then 'turned' by Castro into shooting JFK!"

"What really happened is that the CIA's William Harvey calls Robert Maheu in 1963, who contacts Johnny Roselli and asks him to form a Mafia-CIA hit team to go after Fidel Castro. But the KGB is protecting Castro and the plot fails. The CIA then assigns that same team to take out JFK. The assassination is originally planned for Chicago, and the Mafia uses two shooters out of Giancana's Chicago Outfit, James Files and Chuck Niccoletti, who have had previous assignments with the White Knights in Laos and Alpha 66 in Central America."

"Yes, Mr. President, that's the same Robert Maheu who makes a last-minute change in Robert Kennedy's security guard at the Ambassador Hotel in Los Angeles five years later in 1968. The Mexican guard stands directly behind RFK, and the pathologist later confirms that all three RFK shots came from behind – from less than three inches away, as analyzed by Dr. Cyril Wecht, due to the powder burns. Do you see a pattern here?"

"The JFK assassination plans shift to Dallas when the November 2, 1963 Chicago plans fail, as described by Secret Service Agent Abraham Bolden, who is later arrested, tortured, and jailed when he tried to inform the Warren Commission of the attempted Chicago assassination!"

"I may be mistaken – I grew up in Chicago, but it's been 50 years – I remember a Chicago newspaper article describing a rental car with four rifles in the trunk – purportedly rented by a Lee Oswald – was Oswald also going to be the Chicago patsy?"

"A man named Thomas Arthur Vallee has also been described as a more likely patsy – was Oswald a backup patsy? The Chicago records, which kept the names of two shooters anonymous, (one name was described as Hispanic sounding) were then destroyed by the Secret Service prior to the 1995 ARRB request for records!"

"That's right, Mr. President – both of Oswald's attempts to warn authorities about a planned JFK assassination, first in Chicago and then in Dallas, were destroyed by the FBI – even the names of the shooters in Chicago were ordered classified and then destroyed!"

"The CIA's David Atlee Phillips (AKA Maurice Bishop) is the Controller for both Oswald, the unsuspecting decoy in the Texas School Depository, and Chuck Niccoletti, the actual shooter on the second floor of the Dal-Tex building. James Files is assigned to the Grassy Knoll."

"No, Mr. President, Oswald didn't kill Officer J. D. Tippit either. Tippit attends a special meeting one week before the assassination – that's public knowledge now. Giancana relates that Tippit was supposed to kill Oswald acting as a policeman in the line of duty. Tippit says goodbye to his family on the morning of November 22, and tells them that no matter what happens, that he loves them."

"Oswald gets suspicious that he's the patsy when a police officer draws a gun on him, as he stands next to a witness, on the second floor of the Depository. Oswald was supposed to head to Redbird airport where pilot David Ferry awaits in his plane for a long-promised trip to Mexico – but with the JFK assassination, Oswald's now suspicious that he's the patsy."

"Oswald instead goes to his Oak Cliff rental house, then goes to hide at the Texas Theater. A police car toots it's horn outside of Oswald's rental house after the assassination, but Oswald doesn't answer."

"Now there's a massive manhunt for Oswald-complete with a kill order! The last thing they want is a trial, which might expose Oswald's FBI informant and CIA operative files – they're hunting for him like he's Jason Bourne!"

"Officer Tippit is ordered to the Oak Cliff area, outside of his district. He is animated and angry as he mistakenly stops a car in the Oak Cliff area, and checks the back seat as he looks for Oswald. Officer Tippit then stops another man on foot, a CIA operative, who is also looking for Oswald, perhaps even mistaking the operative for Oswald. The operative talks to Tippit but cannot give away his true identity. To add to the confusion, several CIA operatives are Oswald impersonators who are carrying phony Oswald ID cards!"

"Now, everybody has orders to kill Oswald – he's the patsy! Tippit angrily gets out of his car to further confront the man, who refuses to show his identity. The operative, who is now in danger of being mistaken for Oswald, fires across the hood of the car and kills Tippit, as he exclaims, 'Poor dumb cop!' The CIA operative, who is out of Chicago and a boyhood friend of Files, later tells Files that 'there was a screw-up and I had to kill a cop!'"

"No, Mr. President – we didn't have anything against Oswald – he was a loyal soldier. He 'defected' to Russia on a special project, and he created the Fair Play for Cuba Committee, of which he was the only member! We were planning to blame Russia or even Cuba for the JFK assassination!"

"It's just that every once in a while the Intel Boys have to sacrifice one of their own – it's dirty business and we feel bad about it, but it's for the Greater Good!"

"The point of this story, Mr. President, is that no matter how well you plan an assassination, things can go wrong. The solution was simple – blame Oswald for killing Tippit too! In fact, one notable lawyer, David Belin, ridiculously makes the claim that Tippit's murder is further proof that Oswald killed JFK! I don't know if Belin was really that gullible or naïve, but he did provide us with two contrived explanations for the JFK and Tippit assassinations that he was able to sell to the Warren Commission!"

"I mean, all Belin had to do was talk to the Parkland surgeon, Dr. Charles Crenshaw, about the baseball sized exit wound on the back of JFK's head to know that there was a Grassy Knoll shot, as reported by witness Bill Newman at the Grassy Koll, who fell to the ground with his family and was never interviewed by the Warren Commission!"

"The House Select Committee on Assassinations in 1978 later uses echo location with acoustics analysis of the police dictabelt tape, and localizes this shot to the corner of the picket fence at the Grassy Knoll. With two shot locations, the last government investigation into the JFK assassination concludes there was a 'probable conspiracy'!"

"Why does the CIA use the Mafia? Very simple, Mr. President – the CIA's charter does not allow them to perform domestic assassinations, so they use the Mafia. That also keeps the CIA at arm's length from any involvement. That way, investigators like Robert Blakey can blame the Mafia and get the CIA off the hook!"

"No, Mr. President, the Mafia never orders a Presidential assassination. The Mafia takes orders from the CIA – that protects them from an honest investigation! From Huey Long to FDR to JFK to MLK to RFK the true assassins were never caught, unless they confessed years later like James Files for JFK."

"The Mafia may brag about these exploits, but they've got an insurance policy – the CIA will run interference for them in order to protect their 'assets'! They'll even run counter stories that claim their innocence!"

"Now, Mr. President, the most important thing about these assassinations is that the American people must never be told about them – it would undermine their trust in government! Let the people be satisfied with lone gunmen! Let them name airports, aircraft carriers, football stadiums, art centers, and libraries after the Kennedys, Lincoln, FDR--even Huey Long or Charles Lindbergh, for God's sake. Just don't tell the truth!"

"That was the problem with journalist Dorothy Kilgallen – an Irish catholic born in Chicago who loved JFK – she was the canary in the coal mine! She befriends Jack Ruby during his 1965 trial – in a private interview he spills the beans! She finds out the CIA gave Oswald to the Mafia as the patsy – Ruby even tells her that the conspiracy goes all the way to the top – we're talking LBJ! Ruby earlier tried to tell his story to a visiting Chief Justice, Earl Warren, but he refused to listen!"

"Jack Ruby, who was previously associated with Al Capone in Chicago, was involved with police plans to kill Oswald in Dallas. Ruby then got blamed when the police – many of whom he knew personally – failed to shoot Oswald, so Ruby gets the assignment-he wasn't happy about that! We couldn't let Oswald survive – that would mean a trial and we'd have to release all of Oswald's FBI informant and CIA agency files! We felt bad about suiciding Dorothy, but she was planning to go public, for God's sake!"

"I like to think of myself, Mr. President, as the Catcher in the Rye – the General Public are like innocent children, playing in the rye field. But they don't see the cliff – the Abyss – that lies just beyond!"

"Every once in a while, a child wanders near the Abyss – and it's my job to shepherd him away – to protect our country from disaster! I sometimes wake up at night screaming, as a child nears the Abyss, fearing that I might fail! We must protect the children, Mr. President! I must protect the people from their errant ways! That's why my friends call me, 'The Catcher'!"

"You know, Mr. President, I was a physics major in college. Physics says the world will end in one of two ways – either the Big Crunch or the Big Freeze. Our job in the Intel community is to keep society between the Big Crunch and the Big Freeze! Physics also says that 80% of the universe is made up of Dark Matter – you don't see it, but it controls the world around us."

"Now the Intel community, Mr. President, is a lot like the Dark Matter – in fact, we are the Dark Matter! You don't see us, but we control and protect society – we're the reasons democracies are successful! Do you really think that democracies are always going to pick the right leader? Of course not – that's when we step in!"

"Yes, I know, Mr. President – that's not how democracies are supposed to work! But, throughout history, the role of the Priest, the Elder, the King has been accepted – just like Moses led his people out of the Wilderness – the people need someone to guide them, give them advice – to point them in the right direction!"

"The JFK assassination was a watershed event – we had to send a bold message to future Presidents. We had to let them know that we were now calling the shots, that with our vast array of career diplomats, lettered agencies, and news media infiltration, we were now in control – we could now hide whatever we wanted to keep secret—we were pulling the strings behind the curtain, Mr. President, for we know what's best for the country!"

"Mr. President, we're all going to die someday – the goal is to die with honor. Take Franklin Roosevelt – we gave him an honorable death – he was a great President, up until the end, when he got too friendly with Joe Stalin. He died a private death, with dignity."

"On the other hand, the John Kennedy assassination was more like a public execution – we wanted to send a message to all future Presidents that we were in charge. That's how Jesus wanted it!"

"No, Mr. President – not Jesus Christ. I mean James Jesus Angleton, head of Wet Works, though he had to get approval from William Harvey and our ex-Chief, Allen Dulles. In fact, Dulles got to sign off on two Presidents eighteen years apart – three if you count RFK, who was favored to win – what a career!"

"Sure, Mr. President, they made JFK a hero, but we sent a message to all future Presidents that if they disagreed with the Intel Boys, we would go behind their backs, or we would finish them off one way or another – either with a bullet or a typewriter! We've got those social media folks under our thumbs, too – what a bunch of political zealots! We've got six ways from Sunday to harass a President!"

"That's why we'll never let them solve the JFK assassination – or the RFK assassination, for that matter-it would take away our leverage against future Presidents! We've got to send them a message – let them know who's in charge!"

"So, be careful, Mr. President – watch where you tread!"

"Yes, I know, Mr. President – we promised to release all the records and tell the truth after 50 years – but we've got our pride you know! Besides, we've got to protect our assets!"

"It's the same thing with those damned aliens, Mr. President. JFK was pushing for alien disclosure-which he knew about since his trip to post-war Germany in 1945 with James Forrestal. But if we let the American people see one damned alien, like a Reptilian or, even worse, an Insectoid that looks like a praying mantis – those damned things live forever-then the cat's out of the bag!"

"People will realize they've been lied to, that our universe is much more diverse, our physics and history books are wrong, and that our place in the universe is much smaller than we expected! And we can't have that, Mr. President!"

"Just like Galileo in 1610 at the University of Padua who taught heliocentrism and Professor J. Allen Hynek at Northwestern in 1967 who headed the Air Force's Project Bluebook on UFOs, we can't have these damned astronomers spilling the beans to their students!"

"Telling one secret is like creating a leak in the dam – if the secrets keep leaking out, pretty soon the whole dam will break, and I'll be damned if we're going to let that happen! People must be kept in the dark – away from the Abyss!"

ANALYSIS OF THE JFK BACK WOUND

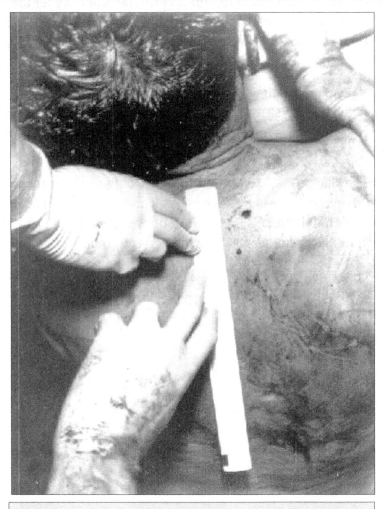

THE JFK AUTOPSY PHOTO SHOWING THE BACK WOUND ENTRY.

NOTE THAT THE LARGE, BASEBALL SIZED, EXIT WOUND IN THE BACK OF JFK'S HEAD, AS DESCRIBED TO ME BY THE DALLAS PARKLAND SURGEON, DR. CHARLES CRENSHAW, HAS BEEN "BLACKED OUT". SECRET SERVICE AGENT, CLINT HILL, ALSO RELATED THAT "THE RIGHT REAR PORTION OF THE HEAD WAS GONE AND WAS IN THE BACK SEAT!"

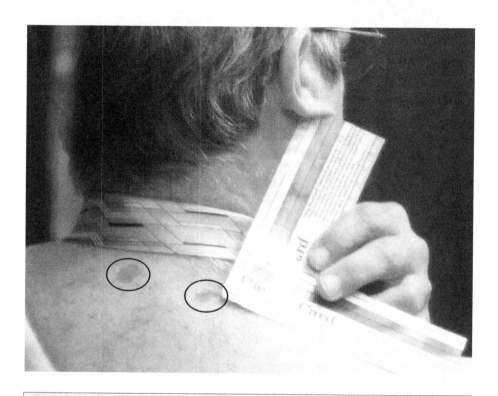

I HAVE PLACED A RED DOT ON MY UPPER SHOULDER AT THE CORNER OF A RULER THAT MEASURES 14 CM FROM THE STYLOMASTOID FORAMEN AND 14 CM FROM THE ACROMION PROCESS, AS MEASURED BY THE BETHESDA PATHOLOGISTS. TWO INCHES TO THE LEFT OF THIS RED DOT IS ANOTHER RED DOT PLACED AT C7 – THE MIDLINE "NOTCH" YOU CAN FEEL IN THE BACK OF YOUR NECK BELOW YOUR NECK TIE OR COLLAR.

THIS ARGUES THAT THE JFK BACK WOUND ENTERS AT THE C7 LEVEL, TRAVELS DOWNWARD TO NICK THE TRANSVERSE PROCESS AT T1, SEEN ON X-RAY, THEN EXITS AT THE STERNAL NOTCH AT T2. THE BULLET NEVER STRIKES SIGNIFICANT BONE, LEAVING A SMALL EXIT WOUND AT THE THROAT.

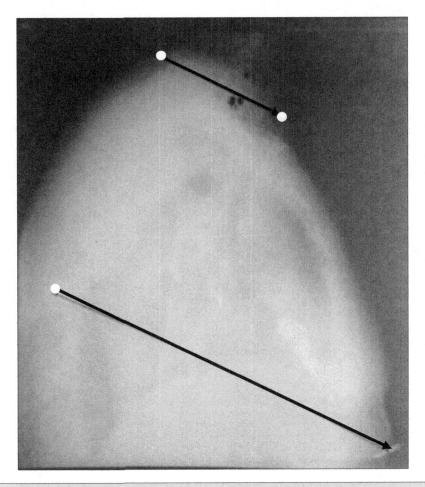

I TAPED COINS ON MY BODY AT THE CORRESPONDING ENTRANCE AND EXIT WOUNDS OF THE JFK NECK WOUND (UPPER LINE) AND THE CONNALLY WOUND (LOWER LINE). I THEN TOOK A LATERAL CHEST X-RAY AND DREW A LINE BETWEEN THE EXIT AND ENTRANCE WOUNDS.

JFK'S WOUND ENTERS AT THE RIGHT UPPER BACK AND EXITS AT THE STERNAL NOTCH IN THE NECK. CONNALLY'S WOUND ENTERS AT THE RIGHT ARMPIT AND EXITS JUST BELOW THE RIGHT NIPPLE.

NOTE THAT THE TWO TRAJECTORIES ARE PARALLEL, SUGGESTING THAT THEY WERE FIRED FROM THE SAME LOCATION AT SIMILAR TIMES FROM THE REAR. THIS ARGUES THAT THE JFK NECK WOUND AND THE CONNALLY ANTERIOR CHEST WOUND WERE BOTH EXIT WOUNDS FROM AN ELEVATED REAR LOCATION.

NOTE: MOTORCYCLE OFFICER HARGIS BEHIND AND TO THE LEFT OF JFK HAS FRAGMENTS OF BONE EMBEDDED IN HIS VEST AFTER THE ASSASSINATION!

SECRET SERVICE AGENT, CLINT HILL, WHO IS SEEN STANDING ON THE LEFT RUNNING BOARD OF THE TRAILING CAR, STATED THAT "THE BACK OF THE HEAD WAS GONE" AFTER THE ASSASSINATION.

THE "GRASSY KNOLL" IS TO THE RIGHT AND FRONT OF JFK.

NOTE: MOTORCYCLE OFFICER HARGIS BEHIND AND TO THE LEFT OF JFK HAS FRAGMENTS OF BONE EMBEDDED IN HIS VEST AFTER THE ASSASSINATION!

SECRET SERVICE AGENT, CLINT HILL, WHO IS SEEN STANDING ON THE LEFT RUNNING BOARD OF THE TRAILING CAR, STATED THAT "THE BACK OF THE HEAD WAS GONE" AFTER THE ASSASSINATION.

THE "GRASSY KNOLL" IS TO THE RIGHT AND FRONT OF JFK.

REGISTRATION

LHO 1939 - 1963
1st Annual
LEE HARVEY
OSWALD
Conference
"Summer of Secrets"

Bill Truels and Judyth Vary Baker

Bill Truels and Madelaine Brown

Dealey Plaza witness Jean Hill and Jim Marrs, 1992

Dr. Cyril Wecht, who challenged the Warren Commission findings, and Dr. Bill Truels (Bob Groden is seated to the left)

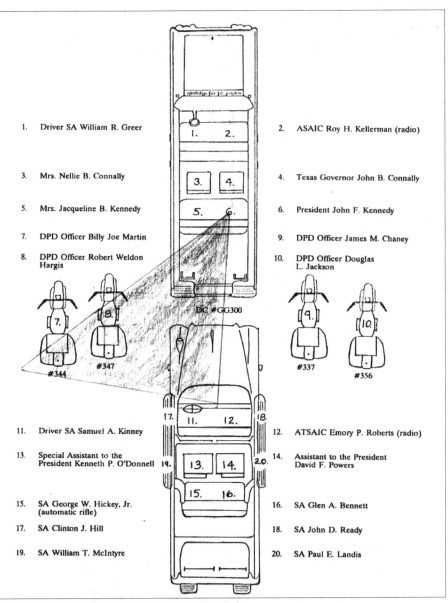

1. Driver SA William R. Greer
2. ASAIC Roy H. Kellerman (radio)
3. Mrs. Nellie B. Connally
4. Texas Governor John B. Connally
5. Mrs. Jacqueline B. Kennedy
6. President John F. Kennedy
7. DPD Officer Billy Joe Martin
9. DPD Officer James M. Chaney
8. DPD Officer Robert Weldon Hargis
10. DPD Officer Douglas L. Jackson

DC #GG300

#344 #347 #337 #356

11. Driver SA Samuel A. Kinney
12. ATSAIC Emory P. Roberts (radio)
13. Special Assistant to the President Kenneth P. O'Donnell
14. Assistant to the President David F. Powers
15. SA George W. Hickey, Jr. (automatic rifle)
16. SA Glen A. Bennett
17. SA Clinton J. Hill
18. SA John D. Ready
19. SA William T. McIntyre
20. SA Paul E. Landis

DIAGRAM FROM *PICTURES OF THE PAIN*, RICHARD TRASK, 1994

I HAVE DRAWN THE SPLATTER PATTERN OF THE JFK HEAD SHOT FROM GRASSY KNOLL, LOCATED TO THE FRONT AND RIGHT OF JFK. FRAGMENTS OF BONE WERE EMBEDDED TO THE LEFT AND REAR OF JFK, IN OFFICER HARGIS' VEST ON MOTORCYCLE #8!

The Picket Fence: Before and After

DISCUSSION
UNLIMITED INC.
presents

THE WARREN REPORT: THE WHOLE TRUTH?

MR. MARK LANE, Attorney and former New York State Assemblyman, does not accept the findings of the Warren Commission Report and will present a critical analysis of the Report.

A PANEL OF PROMINENT ATTORNEYS WILL CROSS-EXAMINE MR. LANE:

MR. JOSEPH A. BALL, attorney for Warren Commission during the investigation.

MR. HERMAN F. SELVIN, former president L.A. County Bar Association.

MR. A. L. WIRIN, noted civil liberties and constitutional attorney.

8:00 P.M., Friday, December 4, 1964
Beverly Hills High School Auditorium
241 So. Moreno Drive, Beverly Hills

Admission: $1.50   Students: $1.00
For ticket information call NO 3-0424

Thus, did the People trust their Leaders –
But the Leaders stubbornly refused to tell the People!
For great was the Secret, and deep were its' Roots!
And the Mystery did remain!

EXTRATERRESTRIALS

"Mr. President, you may think you've heard it all, but what you're about to hear next has caused some Presidents to want to jump out the window!"

"Let me begin by telling you what I learned over 50 years ago, so this is nothing new. My astronomy professor at Northwestern University in 1967 was a man named Dr. J. Allen Hynek."

"Yes, that's right – he was known as a debunker over UFOs and used the term 'Swamp Gas' in 1966 to debunk some Exeter, Michigan UFOs. I will say, in his defense, that was blown totally out of proportion!"

"Dr. Hynek had started his Air Force career working on a top-secret project called the 'proximity fuse' – only the Manhattan Project for the atomic bomb was more secret. The proximity fuse was screwed onto the end of an artillery shell on the Pacific battleships, and used a miniature radar that was designed to blow up at the precise moment that it was near a Japanese Zero. It was so effective that the Japanese had to resort to kamikaze pilots to attack Allied ships!"

"So, Dr. Hynek was no dummy and had the highest military security clearance. When he leaves the Air Force, he becomes the civilian coordinator, first for Project Sign, then Project Grudge, then Project Bluebook, which was the Air Force plan for dealing with UFO reports."

"That's right – he becomes the official debunker of UFOs for the Air Force, but this allows him access to all the top-secret incidents involving UFOs – he gets to see the real UFO incidents, then pass them upstairs!"

"In his book, *The Hynek UFO Report*, Dr. Hynek relates his gradual transformation from a debunker to a believer in the late sixties."

"Well, the first thing Dr. Hynek does in my astronomy class at Northwestern in the spring of 1967 is to pull out a card from his wallet and place it on the horizontal projector in the Tech auditorium, which holds over 400 students. This card is a military access pass that, in the event of a UFO landing, allows Dr. Hynek access to the alien landing site – just like in the movie, 'The Day the Earth Stood Still'!"

"That's right, Mr. President – the military is well aware that some of these UFO reports are real – not a weather balloon, or ball lightning, or the planet Venus or a temperature inversion. They just don't want to tell the public!"

"Why not tell the public? Well, all hell could break loose, Mr. President – if we tell people that aliens exist, it might challenge their religious beliefs, for God's sake, and we can't have that!"

"The extraterrestrials believe that there is a God within all of us, since we all came from one Universal Creator – we're all part of some collective consciousness that includes all religions. The Vatican even houses alien artifacts – the Pope is quite open about all this – he's offered to baptize any extraterrestrial that wishes to become Catholic!"

"But besides religious issues, we're back-engineering some of this technology – lasers, printed circuits, fiber optics, night vision, zero-point energy devices, particle beam weapons – if the aliens don't exist, we don't have to pay them – just like the Indians! But we can't have the oil industry go bankrupt over some of these new zero-point free energy devices!"

"These UFOs are so secret that NASA even censors the Apollo astronaut conversations. Now, Neil Armstrong is getting ready to land on the moon in 1969, and what does he see but six giant alien ships floating on the edge of the crater where he's supposed to land! There's a computer malfunction, so he takes over manual control of the Lunar Lander and nearly runs out of fuel trying to pick a clear landing site!"

"The official word is that two minutes of taped conversation were lost. Armstrong switches to the classified medical channel and states, 'My God, those crafts are enormous!' He wants to tell the world what he saw, but the Intel boys threaten him with the silent treatment – you know, six feet underground, things can get awfully silent! Besides, Neil wasn't the first man on the moon – more about that later!"

"I suspect that the extraterrestrials weren't that happy to see our peace-loving civilization, with over 100 wars in progress at any given time, start claiming the moon! Maybe we needed to grow up a little first!"

"Yes, Mr. President, the existence of extraterrestrials is the most important fact in human history, but don't get your panties in a knot!"

"Think about it for a minute. These UFOs travel at impossibly high speeds, make 90-degree sharp turns at 1,000 G, and neutralize our attempts to shoot them down!"

"Yes, Mr. President, we're still trying to shoot them down! Why? Because they're on our turf! The people must never know that their government isn't in charge! It would undermine their trust in the military, and we can't allow that, Mr. President!"

"Yes, Dr. Hynek talked about the Roswell, New Mexico UFO crash in 1947 and said it was 'significant' and he talked about the Betty and Barney Hill abduction and said it was 'significant.' He talked about UFOs hanging around nuclear missile launch sites at Malmstrom AFB in Montana, as if we humans were being monitored for our destructive tendencies! Why, in some cases, they even fired a laser beam that melted the circuit boards! They did the same thing to the Russian missiles!"

"I turned to the activist student next to me and breathlessly told him that this was the most significant event in human history. He looked at me and said, 'I'm more interested in attending the anti-war rally this afternoon in Deering Meadow!'"

"Dr. Hynek went on to describe four types of aliens, as described by eyewitnesses. There were the Nordics, who were tall and looked a lot like Scandinavians with blond hair and blue eyes. There were the Grays – about four feet tall with large heads, and polydactyly – more than five fingers and toes – and arachnodactyly – very long fingers, like E.T. This material was even included on multiple choice questions for the final exam!"

"In fact, Dr. Hynek was the consultant for the movies *E.T.* and *Close Encounters of the Third Kind* for Stephen Spielberg. Many of the scenes depicted in *Close Encounters* were based on events that Dr. Hynek described in my astronomy class!"

"Then Dr. Hynek described Reptilians with scaly skin and vertical pupils. Finally, he described eight feet tall insectoid types that resembled a praying mantis, complete with a triangular head and mandibles, and more intelligent than humans!"

"But it gets even more weird, Mr. President. Dr. Hynek talked about Beings and their craft going in and out of our third dimensional world and communicating by telepathy. He talked about antigravity devices and traveling through portals of space and time. He introduced the term, 'high strangeness' to describe some beings that don't look at all human, some that live in water, and others that travel without a spaceship!"

"Yes, Mr. President, some of these aliens can fly – you know, gravity is not a true force – Einstein showed that gravity was an alteration in space-time. Gravity actually slows time – and you don't really fall to earth – it's the Earth that's coming up to meet you! That's how those crazy physicists explain it!"

"Ten years later, I attended a lecture by Dr. Hynek in Tulsa, Oklahoma. He showed us his Geiger Counter and how some of these crop circles were radioactive. Yet the official government position was that these crop circles were artificially made by pranksters stomping around in the corn fields!"

"Now, the Intel boys weren't too happy about Dr. Hynek – they weren't sure about what to do about the Nutty Professor. They ended Project Blue Book in 1969 and told pilots to stop reporting these encounters or they would lose their flight status! They even thought about giving Dr. Hynek the Galileo treatment."

"That's right, Mr. President. Galileo was an Italian professor of astronomy in the 1600's who went around preaching to his students that the sun was the center of the solar system, based on the work of Copernicus in Poland before him and others. That way, planets didn't have to stop and reverse their direction, in order to explain their observed motion – and you could explain the phases of Venus – the scholars all knew he was right."

"Why do you think they burned the library in Alexandria, Mr. President? The Greek astronomer Aristarchus of Samos talked about heliocentrism, but his works disappeared. History, Mr. President, is written by the victors. Science and history are just a confabulation of the elites!"

"The Catholic church maintained that Galileo's views conflicted with religious doctrine. Who knows – maybe with that burning Sun placed at the center of the solar system they were afraid the people would go back to worshiping Zeus or Apollo or Helios, like those pagan Sumerians, Greeks and Romans!"

"Anyway, the Inquisition forced Galileo to plead guilty to heresy, in order to avoid being burned at the stake, and sentenced him to house arrest for the last ten years of his life!"

"Now, I can tell you, Mr. President, we don't do that kind of stuff anymore. While it's true that one of the Roswell witnesses had to be shot because he tried to talk, and one of the Roswell aliens was shot at the crash scene when he tried to run away, as described by Colonel Corso, we have found that ridicule is a much more humane way to treat UFO witnesses. We call it Operation Ridicule."

"Ridicule is very important, Mr. President. It may sound cruel, but sometimes you have to ridicule the truth in order to promote the lie. As long as you don't sit next to a Reptilian or a Gray, or even a Nordic, for that matter, and prove to the American people that these entities really exist, like Barack Obama tried to do in 2009 when he received his Nobel Peace prize, then we can safely ridicule the truth tellers!"

"The same thing goes for science, Mr. President. As long as you don't reveal the existence of antigravity craft or electromagnetic propulsion or anti-matter drives, then we can make fun of the truth tellers and their crazy conspiracy theories!"

"The Vatican even was given a device called the chronovisor that allows a person to travel back into history or forward into the future-one Catholic priest actually went back and viewed the crucifixion of Christ!"

"The important thing, Mr. President, is to keep people in the dark – muffle the science and the history – my God, these textbooks and professors are 100 years out of date! The problem with revealing the truth, Mr. President, is that the American people will finally realize that they've been lied to by our universities, our politicians, and perhaps even our theologians! People would lose faith in their government!"

"With full disclosure, Americans would learn the true motive behind Operation Paperclip. They would learn about the German antigravity machines and their alliance with the Reptilians! We had to overrule President Eisenhower, who trusted the Nordic extraterrestrials more than the Reptilians, who promised enormous military gains in return for a few special favors!"

"You know, Hitler and Eva Braun actually escaped to Argentina in one of those Haunebu flying machines. Those badly burned bodies outside his bunker in Berlin were just a ruse. We could have tracked them down, but that was part of the deal! Hoover was ordered to stand down!"

"Tell the truth, Mr. President? That human beings – Earthlings – aren't the center of the universe? The people could never handle that – they might even go bonkers, Mr. President. They're not as smart as you think! Think of all the scientists finding out that the laws of physics, which they worship as immutable, are just a special case! Think of all the religious leaders who claim their religion is the only true path to God!"

"On the other hand, it's been reported that the Earth has over 4,000 religions! So, what's a few thousand more religions?"

"Our rulers are still stuck in the Ptolemaic belief that we humans are the center of the universe – the idea that extraterrestrials walk among us and travel among the stars is special knowledge that must be squelched! The establishment also fears their day of reckoning – what ethical compromises did they make with certain alien groups to obtain antigravity technology and time travel?"

"Now, in the case of first responders – police and firemen – we have placed a chapter in their operational manuals for how to handle a UFO landing or crash incident – they're the first ones on the scene you know. We caution them that their electrical equipment – even their truck engine and pumpers – may malfunction due to the surrounding electromagnetic field. They're told to secure the area to keep witnesses away!"

"We caution them about radioactivity, and about administering first aid, because, depending on the species, the usual first aid measures, such as using iodine as an antiseptic, can be fatal. Crash team whistleblower, Clifford Stone, describes a first aid manual on all the alien types – 57 by last count – and where they're from, so that's why it's important that the military be notified immediately, so we can send in our crash recovery team and shoot – I mean, silence the witnesses!"

"You want to hear something funny? Well, a bunch of firemen in Wilmington, Delaware, answered a call for a plane crash – it turned out to be a UFO! When they figured out how to open the hatch, they found these dead aliens and, you won't believe this – they were only one foot tall! Now, how is that possible – how can you be that small – like a bunch of Lilliputians – and be technologically ahead of us? Go figure! One of the firemen asked if they were supposed to bury these little Beings upside down – like in Gulliver's travels!"

"Now, President John Kennedy wanted to tell the truth – he was for full disclosure. So was Marilyn Monroe – she went around telling people that aliens really exist and that John Kennedy once visited the Beings! We took care of that situation – do you understand what I'm saying, Mr. President?"

"Lately, in a move toward disclosure, the Navy has developed new guidelines for its pilots to report UFO encounters, without fear of ridicule, with vehicles that appear to defy the laws of physics, make 90 degree turns, and outpace our best fighters. Also, the existence of massive underground facilities at our military bases by Northrup, Lockheed, Douglas, and TRW that are developing alternate means of space travel and energy production, should be disclosed to the General Public."

"Full disclosure, Mr. President? I doubt that the Deep State will ever allow that to happen. That film we showed you of President Eisenhower boarding a UFO and meeting with the tall Nordic aliens in 1954 at Edwards Air Force base must never be shown to the public – it would be more damaging than the Zapruder film! Think of the threats to our religions, our way of life if the people on earth found out that we weren't the most advanced Beings in the universe!"

"You know, Mr. President, there's different species of extraterrestrials and they each have their own type of ship. We've captured saucers, pyramidal shapes, spheres and even cubes – they don't have to be aerodynamic because they create their own space-time warp – even their own gravity. There's no sonic boom and they travel just as easily through the air and water. In fact, some of these life forms live in the water – you know, there's a lot more water on most planets than there is land – a lot more space to evolve. But enough about things that don't officially exist!"

"There are basically two groups of aliens, Mr. President. I call them the Shepherds and the Controllers. The Shepherds, from the Pleiades, are part of the Galactic Federation. They believe in non-intervention, destruction of nuclear weapons, the exercise of free will, and internal spiritual growth through meditation, with awareness of a universal consciousness."

"The Controllers, which include Reptilians, as well as Grays from the Orion group, offer more advanced technology in return for universal control, obedience, and yes, a few human lives!"

"The Shepherds promote peace and cooperation – one week before JFK's murder, JFK and Khrushchev had actually agreed upon a joint US-Russia moon program and shared Intel on UFOs, as described by Michael Salla. The Controllers, on the other hand, promote dividing people into warring factions, in order to maintain their dominance!"

"The KGB actually knew about the JFK assassination plans and tried to head them off! As described by author Dick Russel, a double agent named Richard Nagel warned Oswald about being used as a patsy. The KGB was concerned that if the CIA used Oswald as a patsy, with his previous mission to Russia and his one-man Fair Play for Cuba Committee, that Russia and Cuba would be blamed for the JFK assassination! When Oswald refused to heed the warnings and get out of town, the KGB gave Nagel orders to kill Oswald, but he declined to do so!"

"In fact, Nagel even robbed a bank so that he would be in federal custody at the time of the JFK assassination – he wanted to make sure that no one could make him the patsy!"

"The Controllers in the Reptilian collective rely on disruption and war to achieve domination while the Shepherds in the Galactic Federation rely on cohesion and self-edification to achieve unity and peace."

"The Germans during World War II. and later the Americans, courtesy of Operation Paperclip, cast their lot with the Controllers.

Forrestal, JFK, and Eisenhower favored the Shepherds, but were overruled by the military-industrial-alien complex, when MJ-12 signed a treaty behind the President's back in 1954! This was the reason behind Eisenhower's warning against the military-industrial complex in his farewell speech!"

"Yes, Mr. President – you can be overruled – you're just here for a few years – we're here for life!"

"Where's your Cosmic Clearance? No, Mr. President, your clearance is ten levels below Cosmic Clearance – you're not privy to everything that goes on!"

"You see, after World War II., the UFO artifacts all went to Wright-Patterson AFB – that's controlled by the Air Force and answers to the Commander-in-Chief – the President. After all the trouble we had with President Eisenhower in 1954, when he balked at signing a treaty with the Reptilian collective, everything gets moved to Area 51 outside Las Vegas. That's controlled by the CIA, which doesn't answer to the President! Eisenhower even threatened to invade Area 51, which has 40 underground levels!"

"No, you're not just a puppet, Mr. President – you're living flesh!"

"Look – I'll admit that we made a bad decision when we signed with the Draco-Reptilian Orion group – they took more blood-more citizens-more abductions – than we approved. That's what makes full disclosure more difficult – but look at all the technology we've achieved! You can't get something for nothing!"

"The Germans, since the 1930's, had forged an alliance with the Reptilians at their base in Antarctica. After the war, Secretary of the Navy, James Forrestal in August, 1946, commanded Operation Highjump, led by Admiral Richard Byrd, which included thirteen ships and our largest aircraft carrier as part of Task Force 68, to carry out a 'peace mission' to study Neu Schwabenland in Antarctica. They were turned back after only eight weeks in Antarctica, with flying saucers that literally came out of the water-cutting the mission short by six months, with an official report of light losses due to the winter weather!"

"Admiral Byrd's initial press conference, published in the local Chilean newspaper, *El Mercurio*, described large losses of men and planes from an enemy 'with flying objects that could fly pole to pole at incredible speeds.' Byrd was ordered to give no more press conferences, but I can tell you we wanted that same technology, be it from the Germans or the Reptilians or whoever!"

"The President of Northrup, Ben Rich, once famously said, 'We now have the technology to take E.T. home!' Rich also claimed, 'There are two types of UFOs – the ones we build and the ones they build!' Thanks to ships captured after the Battle of Los Angeles, Cape Girardeau and Roswell, we were reverse engineering antigravity vehicles in the early fifties!"

"We also had help from the German scientists after World War II., who had already developed antigravity devices with the help of the Reptilians. It appears that the Apollo astronauts weren't the first men to land on the moon – the Germans got there before the war ended!"

"George H. W. Bush, former CIA director and President, got a big kick out of dressing down the new Presidents, like Barack Obama, at their inauguration, and letting them know the Intel boys were calling the shots – no pun intended, Mr. President!"

"No, I'm not threatening you, Mr. President – just call it a warning. Besides, you don't want to be labeled a Conspiracy Theorist – it wouldn't be good for your reelection, Mr. President!"

"The only thing I don't like about Operation Ridicule is that when full disclosure occurs, the American people are going to be angry at the Intel Boys for tricking them into ridiculing the JFK assassination buffs and the UFO truth tellers. For that reason, Operation Ridicule will actually make it more difficult for the Deep State to finally tell the truth to the American people – when you lie for so long about something, it becomes more difficult to tell the truth!"

"If Americans are ever allowed to see a Reptilian, then the cat's out of the bag – we won't be able to ridicule the truth tellers. So, the Reptilians have agreed to remain out of site, as long as we keep providing live humans. Mr. President – I know this may sound outrageous – but that's what our man Epworth was doing – kidnapping unsuspecting humans – especially children – in exchange for this fantastic technology. There's a price for everything, you know."

"After Epworth got arrested, we had to suicide him in prison – I felt bad about that, but for God's sake, his lawyer announced the previous day that Epworth was going to start naming names, as part of his plea deal!"

"What kind of technology could be worth such a price, Mr. President? Well, for starters, antigravity propulsion – you realize that Einstein showed that gravity is not a true force – it represents an alteration of space-time – you see, gravity slows time. Spaceships are really time travelers!"

"Then there's electrogravitic propulsion using the Biefeld-Brown effect. The Navy has already received a patent for a gravity wave generator – if it's fired at an enemy ship, it creates a space-time warp that fractures the ship – sort of like the Philadelphia Experiment, which involved Robert Oppenheimer and Edward Teller- more than Tesla and Einstein. I will tell you, though, that Einstein's classified work is more significant than his theories of special and general relativity!"

"I can also tell you that the real ship involved in the Philadelphia Experiment was called the *Martha's Vineyard*- a much smaller ship with a single death. That story about Tesla and Einstein trying to make the USS Eldridge destroyer escort disappear in 1943 at the Philadelphia Naval Shipyard, as a cloaking maneuver against the Germans, was a ruse to protect their time travel experiments- as well as Oppenheimer and Teller."

"After full disclosure occurs, they'll have to give out so many Nobel prizes in physics that they'll need a copy machine to print all the certificates!"

"The existence of aliens who walk among us will be a bitter pill for humanity to swallow – worse than Copernicus and Galileo, when people found out that the Earth wasn't the center of the universe."

"You see, with the existence of intelligent aliens of all shapes and sizes, our very social orders, our natural laws – even our religions – are brought into question! Our science books and our history books will have to be rewritten! But perhaps this will be a good thing, as we come closer to knowing our true selves and understanding the world around us!"

"You know, Mr. President, it's kind of funny. The government requires that extraterrestrials register – otherwise they'll get chased down and arrested by the Men in Black. But then the government officially claims they don't exist – now go figure!"

"That's right, Mr. President – when you refuse to admit that a group of people exist, you're treating them like second class citizens – yet this same government claims to be enlightened!"

"Mr. President, you can't be serious – give aliens the right to vote? Just because some of them walk among us and are working to elevate our frequency and be more compassionate to others, doesn't give them the right to vote! It's one thing for an illiterate person to sneak across the Mexican border and get the right to vote – it's totally different for a gifted alien to sneak across the galaxy and get that same right, no matter how well-intentioned!"

"Imagine all those people involved with SETI – spending millions of dollars on the Search for Extraterrestrial Intelligence – waiting for some secret radio message. Do you think someone should tell them?"

"Let me tell you a story, Mr. President, that you won't believe. It's four in the morning and I'm in the casino of the Stardust Hotel in Las Vegas. The Rat Pack has finished their show, and I recognize a girl, who I will call Marsha, who was a classmate at Langley. Well, Marsha walks up to the craps table and, to my shock, relieves the dealer! Then a group of Men in Black arrive and take guard positions around the casino."

"Next, a large group of skinny but tall men and woman arrive, wearing sunglasses. Up close, I can tell they've got these large wraparound eyes that aren't human. They don't walk like we do – they sort of shuffle and they're bent over a bit – and they're surrounded by their own group of personal guards. By now I'm very curious – these people sort of blend in, but then they don't blend in! I decide to hang around."

"They play craps for about an hour and then leave. Marsha leaves the craps table and is relieved by the previous dealer. Marsha acts like she doesn't recognize me, but then I follow her to the concession area. She motions me to sit down and have some coffee."

"What was that all about?" I asked. "Who were those people?"

"'Those were Tall Whites from Area 54', Marsha replied."

"You mean Area 51?" I asked.

"'No – Area 54 – at Indian Springs near Dog Lake. They're helping us reverse engineer crashed UFOs – they get tired of living underground in the desert, so we take them out for a little recreation. They struck a deal with President Eisenhower – actually MJ-12 in 1954 – to help reverse engineer the UFO technology. They like to gamble, just like we do – you know, the laws of chance exist throughout the universe!'"

"'The men are quite arrogant – they look down upon us mere mortals! But they've been contracted to reverse engineer their technology!'"

"'The women are very protective of their children and don't let them near the humans – you're not allowed to touch them! The women love to go shopping and buy bright dresses! Their Mother Ship arrives with each full moon – and leaves with each new moon– something to do with gravity and portals.'"

"No, Mr. President, this information isn't classified. Frank Sinatra knew all about it. But try telling this to someone – it's so preposterous that they won't believe you!"

"You know, you don't have to be a genius to figure out that aliens exist – look at the Great Pyramid of Giza – 2.3 million stones weighing four to sixteen tons each and built in 20 years? That's one stone every five minutes, 24 hours a day, for 20 years! And the distance between each stone is only one hundredth of an inch! You can't even cut stone that accurately with today's tools! And the axis of the pyramid is within three arc seconds, or one twentieth of a degree, of the rotational axis of the earth! Go figure!"

"Watch out for political activists, Mr. President, who are portrayed as lone gunmen – Carl Weiss, Sirhan Sirhan, James Earl Ray, Leon Czolgosz, Charles Guiteau – they'll get you every time! Dr. Carl Weiss, who purportedly shot Huey Long, left his gun in the car! And Lee Oswald was a total set-up – he was on the second floor of the Depository, drinking coffee! You know, Guiteau was a terrible shot – hits Garfield in the arm at point blank range! And they never matched the second bullet, lodged in Garfield's back, with Guiteau's gun – they said they couldn't find it! But I'm giving too much away!"

"It's not really a Murder, Inc. that's against American Presidents. Yes, there is organized opposition and, yes, there is a criminal element in all political parties. But the motivation to remove a President is based on greed, monetary control, lust for power, political rivalry and sometimes just plain jealousy! Both Lincoln and Garfield were Dark Horse candidates who never should have been President! At the time, we thought that removing them was a political necessity – I never said we were perfect! At least, Lincoln and Kennedy got their own aircraft carriers!"

"You know, the way I look at this Mr. President, is that, if you know something the General Public doesn't know – well, that gives you a certain sense of superiority – sort of like you've got the goods on them! You've pulled the wool over their eyes – but that's not all bad – it's for their own good after all! What we do is redefine reality, based on our agenda!"

"I've told my agents to quit smiling while they're lying – if you're lying, you've got to be sincere about it – even better, act angry – the better to denounce the truth! When there's a battle for truth, repeating the falsehood over and over again becomes even more important! If I tell you often enough that 2 + 2 = 5, you'll start believing it too!"

"That Freedom of Information Act, known as FOIA was a real setback. Mr. President, can you imagine allowing people to dig through the National Archives to find out what really happened, instead of trusting our official version of history? We've been forced to create our own false documents!"

"Tell the truth to the American people? Why would you do that, Mr. President? You'd be subjected to ridicule and false charges by the Keepers of the Night! This just isn't the right time – give it another fifty years! Truth is malleable and can be pounded by history into a form that you won't even recognize!"

"Freedom of expression? Yes, you have your first amendment rights. But you also have the right to remain silent – use it wisely, Mr. President! The Inquisition has been replaced by the Deep State. Remember, we have activist judges that can put you in solitary confinement for telling the truth – for exposing the underbelly of the Beast!"

"Think of yourself, Mr. President, as the Boat Master – steering the General Public through troubled waters. Learn to cherish that, as their President, you command their dignity and trust! It's like we're living in Oceania, and I'm your Big Brother! I control your reality!"

"You know, with these modern computers, we can create a President, Mr. President, with all due respect. We can make you a citizen, create an Ivy League college transcript, create a passport, even give you a law license without taking an exam! You can even pick if you want to be a Republican or a Democrat! If you're a radical, we can put you in sheep's clothing! We can target your opponents! All we ask is your loyalty, Mr. President! Is that asking too much?"

"Mr. President, I've got a deal for you! We've arranged for a book publisher to publish your book – and here's the good news – your book advance will be ten times more than the projected sales!"

"No, Mr. President, you don't have to write the book – we've hired a ghost writer to take care of all that – and the Presidential scholars are already on board to verify its validity – they're on the federal dole, you know! You might even get to date one of them, like LBJ!"

"It's very important to get the correct truth in the history books, you know – and we'll write the correct truth for you – right from the President's mouth!"

"We've also set up a Presidential charitable foundation – we've arranged for corporate donors to give charitable donations to the Presidential Freedom Foundation – you'll be on a lifetime salary and all you have to do is give an annual speech – don't worry – we'll write it for you – all you have to do is play along – we'll pull the strings for you!"

"You ask about the trigger points for these assassinations – well, that depends on what century you're in! Trigger points for Presidential assassinations and deaths in the 1800's, from Harrison to Taylor to Buchanan's poisoning, to Lincoln and Garfield all had an anti-Northern domestic bias, based on slavery, reparations, and financial banking issues, and may well have originated from the largest southern city in its day – New Orleans."

"During the 1900's, the trigger point for these assassinations and tragedies involving McKinley, Charles Lindbergh's son, Huey Long, FDR, Joseph Kennedy Jr., John Kennedy, Martin Luther King, Robert Kennedy and John Kennedy Jr. centered around international themes, such as isolationism and perceived weakness on the world stage against first fascism and then communism, as well as international banking issues. These assassination plans originated in Washington, D.C."

"In the twenty-first century, the trigger point for threatened Presidential assassinations centers around the battle between socialism, open borders, and globalism versus protectionism and domestic job creation. New laws allow the creation of foundations which enrich family members of Congress from international donations, ensuring their votes, rather than allowing corrupt political bosses to distribute all the spoils. The plans for these assassinations originate on the global stage."

"In many cases, the role of doctors after a President is injured, has played a role in their demise – either wittingly or unwittingly. From earlier days when arsenic poisoning was in vogue, to later days when wounds were probed, introducing infections, or in the case of Huey Long, with intentionally poor surgical decisions, or in the case of John Kennedy where pathologists were pressured to make a large, baseball sized exit wound in the back of the head simply disappear from their records, the Presidential choice of doctors plays a crucial role in their survival and in the public support for 'lone gunman' explanations – for doctors, too, can be political activists or pressured by the establishment to make false choices!"

"Look how we ridiculed and harassed the pathologist, Dr. Cyril Wecht, who objected to the false conclusions of the Warren Commission, which claimed that all shots came from the rear. Why, even the American Medical Association ridiculed the Parkland surgeon, Dr. Charles Crenshaw, who personally told me he saw an entry wound in the right sideburn and a posterior, baseball sized exit wound in the back of JFK's head with cerebellum falling out! The AMA criticized Dr. Crenshaw and told him that he must be mistaken, because all shots came from the rear! Dr. Crenshaw sued the AMA and settled for an undisclosed amount."

"Princess Diana's doctor? Oh, I can't go there Mr. President! Let's just say that occasionally the CIA does favors for MI6 and vice versa. And you'd have to have a request from someone like Prince Philip. But what kind of French doctor happens upon an accident scene and doesn't send the Princess, who's awake and talking and bleeding internally, from going to the hospital for 40 minutes – then tells the ambulance to drive slowly, then passes a hospital along the way? You don't have to be a brain surgeon to figure that one out!"

"Oh, and one other thing, Mr. President – choose your Vice Presidents wisely – don't pick a compromise candidate who opposes your views on major issues – you're much more likely to be poisoned or shot by lone gunmen! That's a lesson that Lincoln, Harrison, Taylor, Buchanan, McKinley, FDR, and JFK never learned – after all, what's the point of killing a President if the Vice President holds those same views!"

"In the case of FDR, we used his health secrets as blackmail to get Harry Truman (Harry Who?), a staunch anti-communist with 2% of the popular vote, nominated over the perennial pro-communist favorite, Henry Wallace! That practically guaranteed Roosevelt's fate!"

"No, Mr. President, Harry Truman, who was Vice President for only 82 days, wasn't involved, but he heard the rumors. I will tell you that Truman never trusted the Intel boys – and for good reason! After the JFK assassination, Truman wrote that the CIA should be limiting its role to gathering intelligence!"

"Now, don't get your panties in a knot, Mr. President – these cover-ups were all done for Good Reason – to protect the people and guide the Ship of State! The main reason I'm telling you about our past Deeds, Mr. President, is so you'll know the consequences of violating our Trust – there's precedent here for all we do! We're all regular people, don't ya know – we just pretend to be special!"

"You're asking about Jimmy Hoffa, Mr. President? That mystery was solved a long time ago – sometimes the myth overshadows the truth – like Babe Ruth's 'Called Shot' at Wrigley Field in Chicago during the 1932 World Series. Babe Ruth in his autobiography stated that he would never embarrass a pitcher by pointing to center field, where he hit the home run. Rather, he held up one finger after strike one, then two fingers after strike two and then hit the 440 foot home run. But the myth endures that he was pointing to center field, because it's a better story!"

"The same thing goes for the Jimmy Hoffa mystery, Mr. President. You see, Jimmy Hoffa received a commutation by President Richard Nixon on the condition that he not return to the Teamsters Union. He had plenty of money – all had to do was retire! Hoffa then acts like Jimmy Hoffa and violates his commutation! The Justice department goes to Nixon and says, 'What the hell is going on – we spent years putting this guy away!' Hoffa ignores all his warnings. The CIA and former President Nixon now contact Chicago's Giancana for the hit on Hoffa in 1975."

"A Mafia hitman, Irishman Frank Sheeran, who is a close associate and longtime friend of Hoffa, gets the assignment from his boss, Russell Bufalino, and confesses on his deathbed in 2003. A meeting is set up at the Detroit Machus Red Fox Inn, but then a car arrives and the meeting is moved to a nearby house. Sheeran sits in the front passenger seat, Hoffa's usual position, in hopes that Hoffa will get suspicious. But Hoffa gets in the back seat of the car, knowing that his trusted protector, Frank Sheeran is in the car. Sheeran gives the driver directions to the house, further reassuring Hoffa."

"Sheeran then admits to killing Hoffa as he enters the house with two shots to the back of the head. There is a DNA match to a strand of Hoffa's hair in the back of the car and to Hoffa's blood in the carpet padding of the house. Hoffa's body is taken to a funeral home crematorium two minutes away – end of story."

"Sheeran makes the point that he himself would have been killed if he failed to make the hit against one of his closest and most trusted associates."

"But myths surrounding the location of Jimmy Hoffa's body endure, Mr. President, because they make for a better story – and the FBI gets to feign ignorance of any foreknowledge! Every once in a while, the FBI resurrects a new story about Hoffa's disappearance!"

"Mr. President, there's an evil force out there – we're in a battle of Good versus Evil. The universe is not friendly. Everything on Earth – the people, the animals, even the trees are all part of a universal consciousness! Be aware of your surroundings and you will come to know yourself!"

"A trained sniper listens for everything- even the insects! Earth is God's giant experiment, and it's our job to keep it working!"

"But there are rivals, both within and without, who seek to undo us. Our job is to guide the Ship of State, to steady the course – to keep the Evil forces away and protect our planet!"

We must create the Reality
And hide the Duality-
The People must not be told
Of Secrets that we hold!

CREATING THE MATRIX

"You know, I'm not a religious man, Mr. President, but Moses led the people out of the wilderness, and that's exactly what we're doing! We were meant to do this! And did Moses tell all his secrets with God? No, of course not!"

"No, Mr. President, I don't pretend to communicate with God – but there is a Higher Being, and we must respect that!"

"What we've done, Mr. President, is to create a matrix – an artificial reality – to steer the public in the right direction. The idea is to alter the public perception of events in order to shape government policy. The Deep State is an unseen hand that protects the public by shielding them from the unseen truth – the true horror of our existence! Immerse yourself in the destructive element and you will come to know the truth – but do not linger there!"

"You're asking if I'm left wing or right wing? Well, how does a bird fly? It uses both the left wing and right wing to get where it's going! We supported FDR getting the country into World War II. – then we had to terminate him in order to get the Cold War going against Russia!"

"But we couldn't have done it without the journalists bending their ethical standards – true journalists, like Jim Marrs and Dorothy Kilgallen, were the canaries in the coal mine, warning us about trouble ahead – now today's journalists are just parrots in corporate owned cages – but we love them – and we pay 'em!"

"Mr. President, don't sell yourself short – you're the designated leader – think of yourself as the figurehead on the bow of a giant ship, warding off evil spirits like days of old! People look up to you to guide the ship – you're the person they voted for after all!"

"That's true, Mr. President – the figurehead doesn't guide the ship – trust us, your advisors, to do that for you! What's important, here, Mr. President is that the people perceive you to be the one in control – it's very important that you play your roll!"

"We're in a democracy, after all – the people must believe that their votes, their weighted judgment, is what determines policy – not some backroom group of politicians and career strategists who call the real shots and manipulate the voting machines!"

"But crowds can be manipulated, Mr. President. It's the elites who start revolutions and wars!"

"I'm sorry to tell you, Mr. President, that our country is not a true democracy – it's a dictatorship – and you're not the dictator! You're just a figurehead, but an important one!"

"No offense, Mr. President, but our democracy works best with a cognitively challenged President, like FDR in his final term, when the 'Brain Trust' ran things – we're talking about career professionals, not some one or two term politician or general! Even though Harry Hopkins, Soviet Agent #19, turned out to be a communist agent, he still did a damned good job!"

"Now, occasionally we support someone who tells the truth – we don't want people to think we're all a bunch of liars! Part of any disinformation campaign is to tell the truth sandwiched between a bunch of lies. That way, if the truth comes out years later, we can claim that we told the truth, but no one would listen!"

"Mr. President, if we told the truth you'd have to rewrite all the history books, all the science books! We're talking antigravity flying machines that go into outer space, levitation, time warp, teleportation – we all exist at a fundamental frequency, you know-even religious dogma will have to be changed! Why, we've even got a weapon that fires gravity waves that'll destroy a rocket or city with a time warp – like an updated version of the Philadelphia Experiment!"

"Einstein, working with Tesla on classified projects, said it best-people just aren't ready for full disclosure, Mr. President. We've got to protect them from the truth!"

"Cheat an election, Mr. President? That's undemocratic! Besides, it depends what you mean by the word cheat! We don't usually cheat that much – although sometimes we do! Someday, the American people will have to be told that many elections have been cheated, but now's not the time!"

"Take JFK – the boys in Chicago and Dallas and West Virginia got him elected. But then we had to get him unelected when he started being too friendly with the Russians – just like FDR in his final days when he gave away half of Europe, before we could stop him at the little White House in Warm Springs, when Dulles in Switzerland and the OSS home boys arranged a penetrating form of cerebral hemorrhage!"

"Forrestal was a father figure to John Kennedy. Forrestal was always busy trying to make peace with everybody. He helped end World War II by letting the Japanese keep their emperor, which had been a stumbling block. The emperor was just a figurehead, but it worked – we were getting ready to drop the third atomic bomb with the 'demon core' of plutonium when the Japanese surrendered!"

"Forrestal created the Amelia Earhart mystery by covering up her capture and later execution on Saipan by the Japanese when negotiations in France had failed. Those crazy Japanese in 1937 were requesting total military control of the western Pacific! With those two sophisticated Fairchild wing cameras, they knew Earhart was a spy! They were actually able to repair her high-tech twin engine Lockheed Electra Model 10 plane and fly it around! Her passport and a Macy's receipt were later found in a vault on Saipan by an American sailor, then lost by the Navy!"

"Forrestal's idea was to resolve post-war animosity with the Japanese and simply let Earhart's disappearance remain a mystery. That also protected FDR and the military brass for rightfully failing to cut a deal in 1937, although it cost Amelia and her navigator, Fred Noonan's lives! Fred was furious that the Navy didn't rescue them from the Japanese mandated islands – he was able to get a star-fix the night after they crash landed and radioed their exact position to the Lexington aircraft carrier. It took a week for the Japanese to find them!"

"Forrestal was head of Operation Paperclip to recruit the German scientists – Wernher von Braun and his Apollo moon rocket program were just a cover for all the covert German antigravity and electromagnetic flying machines. The Germans had already been to the moon and Mars, for God's sake – thanks to cooperation with those damned Reptilians and the Thule society!"

"But Forrestal knew too much about our negotiations with the aliens and their gravity-defying flying machines. Forrestal, along with JFK, visited those German flying saucers after the German surrender – Foo fighters they called them. Forrestal favored full disclosure of the alien presence and our true position in a universe of advanced and diverse life forms. That was too much for the military-industrial-alien complex and the potential for military superiority with this new technology!"

"Why didn't the Germans win the war? The aliens are required to follow the Rule of Non-intervention – they could advise humans what to do, but humans had to build them. Hitler instead focused on the conventional weapons. American experts admitted that the German tanks were actually better, their planes were better, their machine guns were better, and their rockets were better. The problem is that the Germans were outnumbered – it became a war of attrition!

"Besides, in one sense, the Germans did win the war- they expanded their Antarctica base with the Nacht Waffen into outer space, they expanded into NASA and American defense corporations through Operation Paperclip- they even expanded into the Russian missile programs!"

"You wonder why the Germans, and later the Americans, chose the Reptilians? Because the Nordics said that humanity wasn't ready for such destructive technology – can you imagine that? Eisenhour actually agreed with the Nordics. That's why MJ-12, working with the military-industrial complex, signed the alien agreements behind his back in 1954! But before then, Forrestal, who was the founder and head of MJ-12, and who supported the Nordics, had to be removed!"

"Forrestal – always the peacemaker – was declared mentally incompetent in May, 1949, hospitalized at Bethesda Naval Hospital against his will, and a new security guard placed at his hospital door the night he died made sure that Forrestal would receive a quick exit from the 16th floor. This was truly the day the music died and the Cabal took charge!"

"I object to the way he was killed – thrown out the hospital window – he should have been killed more respectfully – but that's just me!"

"Yes, Mr. President. I supported James Forrestal until I realized that his ideas for peace and harmony were too idealistic in a world of conflict and domination!"

"What did the Reptilians get in return? I can't answer that in full detail, Mr. President. Let me just say that this is an ancient race with human ritual and even sacrifice. Just like the Germans, we were willing to accommodate them in exchange for this fantastic technology!"

"A deal with the devil? Perhaps so, Mr. President – and that's another reason why full disclosure will be so painful! Instead of focusing on differences that divide us, the Nordic extraterrestrials focus on similarities that unite us! They claim we are all sacred and we must learn to focus on the love within us and not the hate that divides us! In the words of Alex Collier, 'Together we are human beings-divided we are slaves!'"

"One group promotes diversity between warring factions in order to maintain their domination, while the other group promotes unification with free will and elevation of society to a higher peaceful plane of existence."

"The Controllers promote Disruptors who create chaos and division to promote change – don't call them riots – we call them disruptions.

My dream is for everybody to own their own boat – I call it a Volksboat. But that's personal."

"What's the universe really like, Mr. President? You can find out for yourself – just get a lawn chair and camp in your back yard for a few days!"

"At first, everything will be peaceful – birds chirping, squirrels scurrying around. At night, you might see a mole emerge from the earth. After three or four days, you begin to conclude that everything is peaceful and in balance."

"Then, suddenly, a hawk swoops down and captures a sparrow for food. A snake slithers up a tree and robs a robin's nest of eggs."

"You begin to realize, Mr. President, that all is not peaceful – there are constant battles for survival all the way up the food chain, and that includes humanity! Someone's got to take control. You get out your gun and take charge. Now, is that so terrible, Mr. President? You can't rely on the peaceful order of things!"

"It's one thing, Mr. President, to tell people that the earth isn't the center of the universe, like Galileo in his astronomy lectures at the University of Padua in 1632. But it's downright earthshaking to tell people that human beings aren't the center of the universe, like Dr. Hynek's astronomy lectures at the University of Northwestern in 1967. I mean, there's Beings that are smarter than us, they've been around longer, they have psychic abilities, and some of them even share our genetic code!"

"Don't you realize, Mr. President – we're the guinea pigs!"

"How do we cover things up? Very simple, Mr. President. Certain people who believe in full disclosure and peaceful coexistence, like JFK and his mentor, James Forrestal, had to be eliminated. Mankind just wasn't ready to assume it's place in a universe of intelligent Beings of all different shapes and sizes!"

"We've got to limit access to the truth tellers – ridicule them, put them in jail on false charges, drag skeletons out of their closet, or kill them if we have to – it's very important to protect the legitimacy of the establishment!"

"There's one other trick up our sleeve, Mr. President. Wernher von Braun warned about this with Carol Rosin. It's called a false flag event. This involves using our saucers and laser weapons against our own citizens in order to simulate an alien invasion. The whole point is to manufacture a crisis to unify the world and create a one world government. The whole idea is to scare people into submission!"

"But don't worry, Mr. President – we'll give you plenty of notice. In fact, if you play your cards right, we might make you the King of the New World Order!"

"We've achieved interstellar travel and nuclear weapons before achieving international peace. That makes us dangerous to anybody watching, Mr. President!"

"Why, the Air Force in 1958 had a plan, called Project A119, to set off a hydrogen bomb on the moon!"

"We have to create what I call 'reality gaps' – news blackouts that appear accidental. Take, for example, one of the greatest moments in American history – the moon landing. Just as Neil Armstrong is about to land, he sees six giant kilometer long alien ships floating on the edge of the crater, with Reptilians standing underneath them. So, what happens? There's a two-minute transmission failure, as Armstrong swings his camera on them, and NASA switches to the medical channel!"

Armstrong states, "Oh, my God, you wouldn't believe it. These babies are huge, sir, enormous. I'm telling you there are other spacecraft out there, lined up on the far side of the crater's edge, sir. They're on the moon, watching us."

"Armstrong later uses Double Speak when he gives a lecture and describes descending into what he describes as an alien environment, but everybody assumes he's talking about the harsh conditions on the moon!"

"Think of it – what a fantastic moment for full disclosure – with the entire world watching! People just don't realize that one of the most important events in world history was edited! And then the original film-the greatest film of all time – was 'accidentally' lost! Isn't it great!"

"The problem with Full Disclosure, Mr. President, isn't that the public will find out about our antigravity craft or free energy devices, or even that aliens exist and walk among us. The problem, Mr. President, is the Galactic Federation – kind of like a United Nations among the planets. They believe in unification – the end of wars – peaceful coexistence, self-improvement, free will, kumbaya, and all that kind of stuff – in the words of Martin Luther King, judging people by the content of their character, not the color of their skin!"

"The Reptilians, on the other hand, believe in social change through disruption, the promotion of diversity and victory through conflict – they assist with our development of weapons of war and rule by domination. Divide and conquer! The Reptilians tear up charters and make their own rules! We in the Deep State look upon the Reptilians as revolutionaries – tear up the Constitution, tear up the Supreme Court and start all over! In return, we show them our gratitude by submitting to their demands! We control the people and the Reptilians control us! We let them perform a few abductions and some genetic experiments. Is that so terrible, Mr. President?"

"You know, Full Disclosure won't be the great panacea that everyone talks about. We fight over countries, but extraterrestrials fight over planets – there's good guys and bad guys, and that's going to be a big disappointment! There're different governments, different religions, different morals – you name it – it's a big mess! We're all fractals of the true Source!"

"With regard to protecting secrets, Mr. President, the Mafia's a little loose about things – they feel like it's OK to divulge a secret once everybody involved has died. But when the government's involved, the Intel Boys say it's never OK to divulge a secret – it's a matter of pride, you know. It's important to protect your assets!"

"That's why you'll never see a satisfactory resolution to the murders of JFK, RFK, MLK, Marilyn Monroe, and so on and so forth! In fact, if a major assassination is not resolved, due to what they call lingering questions, that's probably a tipoff as to who's really behind it! We call it magic-sleight of hand!"

"Kill people? No, Mr. President, we don't like to use that term. Better to say 'eliminate' or 'terminate' or 'wet works' – that sounds better – we're a bit more refined – just think of us like James Bond!"

"Oh, and one more thing, Mr. President. William Tompkins states that the first flag planted on the moon was actually a Masonic flag, courtesy of NASA and Buzz Aldrin. They christened our landing site Tranquility Lodge. Then the astronauts marched back up the Lunar Lander and proceeded to come down the ladder with the American flag! That should tell you something about our priorities!"

"Mr. President, through rotational physics, we can literally alter the fabric of reality. Two contra-rotating magnetic fields can alter gravity and even time itself. Tesla discovered this – so did the Germans in the 1930's. Tesla actually had an electric car in 1920 that ran on zero-point free energy! Someday, they'll have to re-write the physics textbooks – but not until we're ready!"

"Gravity is not a true force – it comes in waves and alters space-time, Mr. President. But it's mostly time that is affected-90% of the altering is with time and only 10% with space – astronauts are really time travelers!"

"Einstein described the dividing line between past, present, and future as an illusion – although a persistent one! Just like our reality, Mr. President – all of the important events in human history involve altered time—we create our own history!"

"Why, we could put you in the Montauk chair, send you back to Dealey Plaza, and you could stop the JFK assassination! But that would create a new timeline, a parallel universe with full disclosure, which we're opposed to!"

"Don't you see the duality, Mr. President? We're only seconds away from the Abyss! It's our job to keep our civilization from going over the edge—into the Heart of Darkness! What we have found is that if we keep repeating something often enough, people will start believing it – we call it the power of persuasion! We must lie to the people to protect them!"

"You know, Mr. President, we nurture and create future Presidents. Liberation movements by their nature require a certain teardown of traditional values before new norms are created. My only fear is that we might create a liberation movement that gets out of control and results in our own destruction! In trying to reform society, we might send it down the abyss! Have we created a monster that might one day destroy us?"

"Yes, Mr. President, I sometimes have second thoughts. One thing that bothers me is that there seems to be an unquenching desire for people to know the truth – I mean, hundreds of years later, people are still searching for historical truth – that concerns me. Why don't people just accept what they're told and move on – life would be a lot simpler for us in the Deep State!"

"It's important, Mr. President, to remember the verbal history I've given you, and to pass it on to the next President – that's our only hope to preserve the true history for the next millennium! History books are written by the victors and will never tell the true story!"

"No, Mr. President, we're not creating an artificial world-we're creating a new reality – a sort of Shangri-La where the expedient explanation surpasses a troubling truth!"

"A day of reckoning? Mr. President, there must never be an attempt to reopen these investigations – it would undermine the people's trust! It's time to move on – let bygones be bygones!"

"This is a great country, Mr. President, but you can still get into trouble for telling the truth!"

"No, Mr. President, I'm not talking down to you – I'm just letting you know that you're not in charge!"

"Mr. President – you can't just storm off! Your life is at stake here!

You're being watched, monitored wherever you go! These aren't Rumors!"

"We're all Catchers in the Rye! Our job is to keep society from going over the Edge – nuclear destruction, biological warfare, worldwide famine – it's all being manipulated and it's closer than you think!"

"We can manufacture riots and disease. We can make you a hero or a chump. People can be manipulated, Mr. President. But it's all for the Greater Good!"

"If you don't join with us and accept the Duality – if you don't trust us to make the right decisions, the Killing of the King Ritual will be acted over yet again!"

"There is a Duality
That denies the Reality --
Accept the lie –
Or prepare to die!"

THE PRESIDENT SPEAKS

"You wish to speak, Mr. President?"

"We must admit our mistakes in order to overcome them. Most of these 'mysteries', from Amelia Earhart to JFK to UFOs, are nothing more than government secrets. We must admit our faults in our search for truth. We must learn to say, 'I'm sorry for my mistakes,' and forgive those who have harmed us. Only then can we achieve a higher plane of existence and take our place among the stars!"

"There are certain things that American people deserve to be told. These are as follows:

1. Senator Huey Long, an isolationist, was shot by his own bodyguards in a plot that had the approval of key members of both parties. Because of an oath he took upon threat of death, the doctor was pressured to throw a punch, but he was not part of the shooting, and was opposed to the shooting.

2. Charles Lindbergh's son was kidnapped and killed on orders from the Intel Boys – Lindbergh, also an isolationist, was too popular to be assassinated. The purported kidnapper, Richard Hauptman, was totally innocent.

3. Amelia Earhart and Fred Noonan were on a spy mission with a souped-up plane from the future Skunkworks boys. They were forced to land in the Marshall Islands on Mili Atoll when the port engine malfunctioned and caught fire, burning Amelia's left arm and shoulder. They were captured by the Japanese and executed when negotiations failed.

4. FDR died in Warm Springs from a .38 caliber bullet to the head that was not self-inflicted. The Cold War was beginning, and FDR was too friendly with the Russians.

5. James Forrestal, who was the head of MJ-12, was assassinated because he was in favor of full disclosure of the extraterrestrial presence.

6. President Kennedy was killed in a CIA-Mafia plot because of his desire to disclose the extraterrestrial presence and restructure our financial system to eliminate Federal Reserve Notes, favored by the bankers – this plot had Vice Presidential approval. Lee Harvey Oswald was an FBI informant and was totally innocent.

7. Senator Robert Kennedy was killed for the same reason by the same forces – this had Presidential approval.

8. Martin Luther King was killed because of his opposition to the Viet Nam war. James Earl Ray was not a shooter.

9. John Kennedy Jr. was killed because he chose to walk in his father's footsteps and run for office – this also had Presidential approval.

10. When American people are finally told that extraterrestrials exist and walk among us, this will begin the great awakening, when humans on earth will assume their rightful place in a diverse universe of thousands of intelligent Beings. This will be the greatest revelation in human history!"

"Around the United States we have created a protective cocoon of disinformation and lies to protect the public from unpleasant truths. The cocoon provides warmth and protection to those who accept its walls. But those who venture outside in a search for truth will be trapped in a fibrous web of ridicule, deplatforming, social rejection, and sometimes even death!"

"For example, Pacific Islanders who grew up in Saipan heard stories of a female aviator and her navigator who were captured, imprisoned on Saipan, and eventually killed prior to the end of World War II. Pacific Islanders are shocked when they visit the United States and are told about the ongoing search for Amelia Earhart and the unsolved mystery of her disappearance around Gardner Island!"

"In the last 75 years there have been tremendous advances in technology that are being shielded from the public. These include so-called free energy devices, antimatter and antigravity propulsion systems, spacecraft that travel among the stars, and over 100 forms of extraterrestrials – some who look just like us and even live among us!"

"Yet this information is withheld from the public, the universities, and most corporations. These advances are being carried out at underground military bases, much like the V1 and V2 rockets that were developed by the Germans during World War II., using underground construction facilities."

"When will the public be allowed to enjoy these advances in medicine that will extend our lifetime, relieve our suffering, and end our energy dependence on oil?"

"There is a message here, Holden Coalfield, that I'd like to relate – people need to stop hating each other and start loving each other. People need to start working together instead of pulling apart – we need to stop all this competition and pull together for the Common Good!"

"This will be the beginning of our integration into the galaxy, into our universe. We must accept all the life forms instead of blocking them out. This will involve a certain humility, a certain realization that we are one of many, and that we don't all look alike or even think alike – but we can still work together for our common needs!"

"Meditate daily and learn the Inner Peace that shapes our actions, and you will come to know yourself!"

Is it possible to Transform
To another Shape or Norm?
Or is it just our Imagination
That creates Transfiguration?

THE TRANSFORMATION

"I noticed, Mr. Coalfield, that when you talked about the James Forrestal and John Kennedy assassinations, your pupils changed – and your skin developed a greenish hue. I even noticed a few scales on the back of your hands!"

"How's that, Mr. President?" Coalfield asked as he turned to look out the window.

"Your pupils turned vertical, like a cat or lizard – are you trying to hide something, Mr. Coalfield?"

"What do you mean?" Coalfield asked as he continued to gaze out the window.

"You're a Reptilian – there's no need to hide it or be ashamed. Turn around, let me have a look!" the President exclaimed. "You told me this meeting was all about honesty."

"Very good, Mr. President," Coalfield replied as he turned to reveal his reptilian face with green, scaly skin and vertical pupils – a truly dramatic transformation!

"I'm not a shape shifter," Coalfield added. "But I can project a human appearance to your brain whenever I wish – the power of suggestion is one of the human weaknesses!"

"You know, Reptilians were on this earth long before the human experiment – we created you as slaves and propagated your species throughout the universe – that's why so many alien forms resemble humans!"

"But we created you – workers who then rebelled against their masters and are throwing us off the planet – how ungrateful! We used you for labor and for food – we kidnapped entire third world villages and exported your best scientists to other worlds!"

"You know, we should have won World War II – we gave Hitler six types of flying machines – saucers if you will. Intergalactic rules prevented us from simply taking over. But Hitler focused on those V1 and V2 rockets instead of the saucers. Do you know the Germans went to the moon and Mars before the war ended? Do you know we gave them bases in Antarctica 1½ miles below the ice, which were accessed by submarine?"

"When Admiral Byrd attacked Antarctica in Operation Highjump in 1946, those Germans – the Nacht Waffen-the Dark Fleet with their flying saucers came out of the water, shot down his entire fleet of planes and sank one ship! But the real victory for the Germans and their Reptilian friends was Operation Paperclip – the exporting of German-Reptilian technology to the United States and Russia – and Antarctica!"

"The Secret Space Command was a true star force, with ships built by the U.S. Navy that could travel through space and time—you know that gravity is more an alteration of time than space!"

"As Undersecretary of the Navy, James Forrestal headed a group of German spies during World War II that relayed German technology secrets to American corporations in an attempt to reverse engineer what the Germans were doing. President Truman later formed MJ12 with Forrestal at the head. Forrestal favored negotiations with the Nordics- not the Reptilians!"

"But the Reptilians offered the same war technology that the Germans had been receiving – the Germans had already been to the moon in 1942! Forrestal, with JFK as his understudy, was getting in the way and had to be removed in 1949. That should have been a warning to JFK to keep his mouth shut about suppressed technology and alien disclosure!"

"You know that Eisenhower in 1952 interviewed six groups of aliens. That's when the Germans, known as the Dark Fleet, the Nacht Waffen, put on a light show with several nights of UFOs above the White House. Like Forrestal, Eisenhower picked the Nordics, but he was overruled by the military-industrial complex, which by now was heavily infiltrated with the Paperclip Germans and their Reptilian allies."

"The Reptilians offered superior, even dangerous technology, in exchange for a few human bodies for experimentation. Once the contract was signed against Eisenhower's wishes, a few human bodies became a lot of human bodies for experimentation and sacrifice by several alien species! This became a large human trafficking operation, run by the Intel Boys!"

"But the Nordics saw the projected future timeline with a Reptilian domination and decided to intervene. The Galactic Federation has been removing negative aliens from the Earth, Moon, and Mars."

"Do you know that when the Project Apollo astronauts landed on the moon in 1969, there were six-kilometer-long Reptilian ships floating at the crater's edge, waiting to greet them? Do you know that NASA has lost the film footage and two minutes of audio from the first astronauts to land on the moon? The alien message was simple – gather a few rocks and go home!"

"Astronauts were sworn to silence and plans for a future moon base were put on indefinite hold. This perhaps best explains why the first man on the moon, despite world adulation, became a recluse – Neil Armstrong possessed earth shaking knowledge that would change our whole view of humanity-yet he could not share it!"

"But humans need to stop blaming Draco Reptilians for all their problems. The Federales cut a deal with the Tall Whites, the KIlly Tokurt, at Area 54 for saucer technology and soul scalping in return for abductions and human trafficking. The Taal Shiar assisted the Federales with the JFK assassination. And those pesky Grays assisted everybody!"

"You know, Mr. President, Reptilians may be forced off planet Earth. But we live in a universe where it's conquer or be conquered. It is a continual battle of good vs evil – there are many hostile groups that seek to dominate. We are all a fractal of the true Source."

"With regard to history, Mr. President, you should know that Reptilians have been on the Earth for six thousand years. We have worked with the elites of every generation to promote division and wars and provide our version of history and science. You should know, Mr. President, that every book that's been printed is misinformation! The educational system does nothing but put people in a mental strait jacket – talk to a University Physics professor about antigravity propulsion and he'll laugh in your face!"

"I wish Earth well, Mr. President, in its battle for compassionate coexistence with the Shepherds, but we live in a universe of conflict and domination – be ready for the Controllers – for we shall rise again!"

"The Earth can only survive, Mr. Coalfield, if we can learn to put aside our differences and work together for the Common Good – we cannot let race, religion, or creed divide us, and we must put an end to the wars that destroy us – only then can we achieve a higher plane of existence and join our extraterrestrial family!"

EPILOGUE: USING COMMON SENSE

Have you ever tried applying Common Sense to American history? Doing so will leave you in a quandary! Here are a few examples:

1. Why did the judge refuse to allow a DNA test at John Wilkes Booth gravesite or allow investigators to check for a fractured leg? Why did Lincoln's doctor pass metal probes into his brain, causing more damage than the bullet, and hastening his demise?

2. Why was Senator Huey Long accidentally shot twice by his own bodyguards after Dr. Carl Weiss threw a punch at Huey Long? Why did Dr. Weiss's gun disappear for 56 years, only to be found in the police chief's daughter's possession? Why did his bullets not match with Huey Long?

3. When sailors aboard the U.S.S. Ward in Pearl Harbor sank a minisub one hour before the Japanese planes attacked, why wasn't the general alarm sounded? Why were the sailors sworn to secrecy? Was this really a 'surprise' attack?

4. Why did three aircraft carriers happen to leave Pearl Harbor only hours before the attack, raising suspicions with Admiral Yamamoto of a counter-attack that caused him to call off a second wave of Japanese Zeroes?

5. Did FDR really contract polio at the unusual age of 39? Why did all his health records, which were placed into a vault at Bethesda hospital, disappear after his death?

6. If FDR died from a stroke or cerebral hemorrhage, why was the left side of his face and neck markedly swollen and disfigured? Why did Eleanor refuse an autopsy? Why did Eleanor insist on a closed casket and refuse to allow Elliott, her son, to return from the Pacific? Why did Eleanor say her husband "died like a soldier"?

7. If Marilyn Monroe died from a massive pill overdose, why was her stomach empty? The coroner had never before seen such a high drug level of chloral hydrate and nembutal in the bloodstream with an empty stomach.

8. When acoustic signals in Dealey Plaza revealed five supersonic rifle shots, why did the government still conclude that only three shots were fired in the JFK assassination?

9. Why does the government deny a Grassy Knoll shot when the last government investigation into the JFK assassination concluded that a frontal shot had been fired from the Grassy Knoll?

10. If JFK Jr., a prospective Presidential candidate, died from spatial disorientation when his plane crashed into the ocean, why were the printed circuits melted in the engine compartment? If there was no fire in the engine compartment, why did he turn off his fuel switch? Why did witnesses initially relate the weather was clear? Why was a fireball reported over the water?

11. Dr. J. Allen Hynek, my Astronomy 101 professor at Northwestern in 1967 and the civilian head of the Air Force's Project Blue Book, described four types of extraterrestrial Beings flying UFOs that can make 90 degree turns. He showed us a card in his wallet that gave him special access in the case of a UFO landing. Why is the public still being told that UFOs and aliens don't exist?

FROM THE AUTHOR

I was born and raised in Chicago, graduated from Northwestern University in 1967, and am a practicing general surgeon in Oklahoma City. My other works include: *Breach of Faith*, a study of the JFK assassination, *Quatrains of Camelot*, an epic poem of the JFK assassination, *Poems From The Heartland*, *Tales From The Doctor's Lounge* – a humorous account of my medical experiences, and *The Lancer Chronicles – Surviving Cancel Culture, Microaggressions, and Content Moderation* – a satirical history of these turbulent times.

Throughout my life, I kept coming across conflicting accounts of major historical events. I attended many JFK assassination conferences over thirty years and personally talked with Dr. Cyril Wecht, Jim Marrs, Robert Groden, Dr. Charles Crenshaw, Dick Russell, Ed Tatro, Vince Palamara, Walt Brown, Judyth Baker, Madelaine Brown, Dealey witness Bill Newman, and many others, who provided an alternate view from the lone gunman explanation.

During my forty years as a general surgeon in Oklahoma City, I scrubbed with one department chairman at Mercy, whose father attended a colorectal conference in 1944 by Dr Frank Lahey in Boston, who provided personal information regarding FDR's prolonged illness.

Another department chairman at Baptist provided a personal account of FDR's traumatic demise. This same story was confirmed to me in my wound clinic with personal knowledge from the Chief of Podiatry at Deaconess Hospital, whose father had received a letter after the war from a former Navy comrade – Roosevelt's personal physician, Dr. Howard Bruenn.

As a student at Northwestern University in the spring of 1967, my Astronomy 101 professor, Dr. J. Allen Hynek, who was the civilian head of the Air Force's Project Blue Book, described four types of aliens, with characteristics such as arachnodactyly and polydactyly. Yet the government officially claimed that flying saucers and aliens didn't exist!

I wrote *Alternate American History 101* in an attempt to resolve these and other historical dilemmas. Perhaps one day, an American President will come forward and release a digital recording of his first Presidential briefing!

Made in the USA
Middletown, DE
03 October 2022

11794199R00076